HUNt

HUNt

Mastering the **Strategies** of
Recruiting Champions

ANIRBAN BISWAS

Hunt: Mastering the Strategies of Recruiting Champions
Anirban Biswas

Copyright © 2024 Anirban Biswas

All rights reserved. No portion of this book may be reproduced, stored in a retrieval system, or transmitted in any form or by any means- electronic, mechanical, photocopying, recording, or other- except for brief quotations in printed reviews, without the permission of the publisher..

TABLE OF CONTENTS

PREFACE ix

INTRODUCTION 1

CHAPTER 1
Creating a Strategic Sourcing Plan 7

CHAPTER 2
Assessing Beyond the Resume 24

CHAPTER 3
Making Data-Driven Decisions 38

CHAPTER 4
Sourcing for Specialized Roles 53

CHAPTER 5
Optimizing Candidate Experience 69

CHAPTER 6
Harnessing Talent Analytics 86

CHAPTER 7
Marketing Your Openings 101

CHAPTER 8
Interviewing to Impress.. 115

CHAPTER 9
Innovative Assessments 127

CHAPTER 10
Building a World-Class Recruiting Program.. 140

CONCLUSION 158

Gratitude:

I want to express my gratitude to my mother, who has always been my source of guidance and inspiration - showing me the importance of determination, compassion, and striving for greatness.

PREFACE

As I sit down to pen this preface, I find myself reflecting on an unexpected journey. I am not a professional writer, nor did I ever envision authoring a book. My journey has been one of passion, dedication, and a deep-seated desire to contribute to a community that has shaped my career and personal growth—the recruiters' community.

Recruitment, at its core, is a form of art. It involves the process of discovering, engaging with, and nurturing individuals with the potential to make an impact on organizations and industries. Throughout my career spanning more than two decades, I have had the privilege of being actively involved in this dynamic field. I have personally witnessed how skilled recruiters can bring changes. Drawing from my range of experiences and the lessons acquired over time, I felt compelled to share my insights in my book titled **"Hunt: Mastering the Strategies of Recruiting Champions.»**

I decided to write this book because I wanted to give back to the community that has supported me greatly. I've had the privilege of learning from industry experts and my goal is to share my experiences and insights to help others succeed in this field. This book is my way of helping others grow and achieve success by passing on the knowledge and strategies that have been crucial in my journey.

In these pages, you will find a blend of case studies, and practical tools designed to enhance your recruiting skills. Whether you are a seasoned professional or just starting in the world of recruitment, this book aims to provide valuable insights that will help you navigate the complexities of recruiting champions.

Join me on this adventure. Let's dive into this book with an open mind and a readiness to discover fresh viewpoints. The realm of hiring is changing constantly. I firmly believe that there's potential for development and enhancement. I trust that "**Hunt**" will be a guide for you assisting you in honing your skills in attracting talent and reaching new heights in your professional journey.

Lastly, I want to express my gratitude the to recruiters. Your hard work, perseverance, and steadfast pursuit of excellence never fail to motivate me. I genuinely hope that this book will serve as a resource in your career helping you achieve success in identifying top talent.

With warmest regards,
Anirban Biswas.

INTRODUCTION

To begin the introduction, let me share a story about a self-made Indian billionaire. In response to a journalist's inquiry about the key to his success, he openly declared, "*It's all about the people. I made it a point to recruit individuals more skilled than myself, and they propelled the organization forward.*" This illustrates the critical role of effective hiring.

At the core of every organization lies the ability to discover and integrate the ideal talent. This forms the theme of this book "*Hunt: Mastering the Strategy of Recruiting Champions.*" Within its pages, I shared time-tested techniques and real-life anecdotes to empower readers in enhancing their talent acquisition prowess. Beyond being a guide on hiring practices, this book delves into the art of identifying and nurturing individuals who possess the potential to elevate your organization to heights.

Undoubtedly, recruiting the people holds significance. It surely cannot be emphasized enough. In his work "*Good to Great*", Jim Collins underscores the role of bringing onboard exceptional individuals as the initial and vital step towards transforming a company from being merely good to truly remarkable. It is not about having plans, processes, or technologies; without skilled and motivated employees to put them into action, they all lose their value. Hence in today's fast-paced and fiercely competitive business landscape, finding top-tier talent stands as an imperative.

Making wrong hiring decisions can have consequences, such as decreased productivity levels, high employee turnover rates, and missed opportunities. In this book, I aim to guide readers through these challenges by going beyond the basics of hiring. This book teaches how to identify, attract, and develop individuals who will not only excel at their jobs but also bring something special to the organization.

The book emphasizes the importance of hiring people for any industry. For instance, Jim Collins in his book "*Good to Great*" states that having people is the initial step towards becoming a great company. Innovative strategies, cutting-edge processes, and advanced technologies are all meaningless without individuals who can implement them effectively. That's why finding and retaining employees holds value in today's competitive business landscape.

Despite this understanding, many companies still struggle with their hiring practices. They often rely heavily on instinct, focus solely on specific skills and past experiences, lack a well-planned interview process, and overlook how well a candidate aligns with their company culture.

Making wrong hiring choices can come at a cost resulting in decreased work performance increased employee turnover and missed opportunities. The purpose of this book is to assist leaders and organizations in overcoming these challenges. It serves as a resource offering guidance on selecting and nurturing individuals who not only excel at their jobs but also contribute to the company's growth and success. These are the individuals who possess skills, motivation, and vision that can propel an organization to new heights.

In essence, this book goes beyond hiring practices. It encourages adopting a more effective approach to team building. It emphasizes the recognition and utilization of potential. Drawing from years of experience, I provide insights and guidance on the journey, toward creating teams that are not just capable but truly outstanding.

Within the pages of "*Hunt*", an encompassing guide awaits those seeking to revolutionize their talent acquisition strategies. This book delves into crafting a recruitment plan that targets candidates while captivating both active job seekers and passive prospects.

The book explores the balance of using technology, such as AI and automation to streamline the sourcing and screening processes in recruitment while still acknowledging the importance of human interaction. It highlights the practices for harnessing technological advancements and emphasizes the need to maintain a personal touch in a digital world. The goal is for technology to enhance rather than replace the human-centered aspects of recruitment.

"*Hunt*" goes into depth about interviewing techniques that go beyond surface-level information found on resumes. It focuses on asking questions and seeking insights to accurately assess both hard skills and nuanced soft skills. The text also delves into evaluating abilities, emotional intelligence, motivation, and other factors that contribute to a candidate's success. This evaluation is conducted using established and validated testing methodologies to ensure an understanding of each candidate's capabilities.

Additionally, the book discusses the design of an interview process that is both structured and conversational. It advocates for a format that uncovers a candidate's behaviors, competencies, and alignment with company culture. This approach helps to peel back the layers of a candidate's persona, revealing their authentic self.

Moreover, this book addresses the critical issue of biased decision-making in hiring. It underscores the importance of incorporating diverse perspectives in the final stages of candidate selection. This ensures a more balanced and fair evaluation process.

The book also presents methodologies for quantifying candidate assessment data. It argues against relying on intuition and advocates for making evidence-based hiring decisions. This approach is grounded in concrete data, steering clear of subjective biases and providing a more objective framework for evaluating potential hires.

In addition, the book highlights the value of continuous improvement in talent acquisition. It encourages the utilization of data analysis and feedback mechanisms to refine and enhance recruitment strategies over time.

The principles and strategies outlined in this book are universally applicable, and applicable to organizations of all sizes and industries. Whether it is recruiting for a startup or an expansive multinational corporation, the ultimate goal remains consistent: identifying, attracting, and selecting individuals who will excel in their roles and make contributions to achieving organizational strategic objectives.

Readers of this book will not only acquire knowledge. They will also develop a transformative mindset equipped with the necessary skills and tools to revolutionize how their organizations approach sourcing, assessing, and integrating top-tier talent.

The book makes a promise to improve the process of hiring employees leading to increased productivity, innovation, and a competitive edge. This guide positions its readers as experts, in finding and recruiting the champions. In today's competition for talent, it is crucial to secure exceptional candidates efficiently and effectively before competitors do.

"Hunt" acts as an expert-led masterclass on recruiting champions. By applying the insights and strategies from this book, readers are poised to elevate their hiring practices, giving them an advantageous position in the competitive business landscape.

CHAPTER I
CREATING A STRATEGIC SOURCING PLAN

KNOW YOUR NEEDS

Accel Technologies, a growing tech startup, found itself at a crossroads. The business was booming, and they were planning to double their workforce within the next year. However, their current recruitment strategies were inefficient, failing to attract the class of talent needed for their ambitious growth.

Eva, the head recruiter at Accel fully grasped the urgency of the situation. Alongside her team, she was overwhelmed with the task of scouring from LinkedIn and various other job boards. Resume databases were narrowing in search of candidates to fill an ever-increasing number of vacancies. Unfortunately, their efforts often fell short. The candidates they found frequently lacked either the skills or the necessary interpersonal abilities required for the roles at hand. The interview process became chaotic as promising candidates accepted other offers, before Accel could make a decision.

Recognizing that a major change was imperative, Eva set out to develop a sourcing plan. This plan aimed to align their recruitment efforts with the company's growth trajectory. Working closely with department leaders, Eva focused on forecasting positions and pinpointing the technical expertise and interpersonal skills essential for success in these roles. Accel took an approach by moving from generic job descriptions, and instead focusing on detailed candidate profiles that truly captured the unique culture and environment of their company.

With these insights in hand, Eva steered the team towards a strategy for finding talent. They started exploring platforms like GitHub and Stack Overflow, where they could find candidates who fit their requirements. The team became skilled at identifying candidates who were already excelling in such roles and approached them with exciting opportunities at Accel. Rather than waiting for applications to come in, they took a proactive approach by building a talent pipeline to meet both present and future needs.

Eva also introduced an interview process. They implemented pre-planned behavioral questions that aimed to uncover candidates' abilities and gauge their compatibility with the company's values. Hiring managers were involved in creating questionnaires tailored to the specific technical and soft skills their departments needed. Interviewers received training on how to delve into candidates' past experiences related to problem-solving, teamwork, and commitment to delivering quality work.

The impact of these changes was remarkable and impressive. In two quarters, Accel successfully made 25 hires, significantly boosting their product development, customer success, and growth operations teams.

After implementing an approach to sourcing, they were able to uncover incredibly talented individuals known as *'purple squirrels'*. These individuals possessed not only technical expertise but also fit in perfectly with the company culture.

Accel successfully achieved its hiring goals within nine months of revamping its talent acquisition process. This accomplishment marked a milestone in the company's expansion. Eva and her team received deserved recognition for orchestrating this turnaround, showcasing their mastery of strategic sourcing. However, Eva understood that this achievement was the beginning. She eagerly looked forward to refining and enhancing Accel's recruitment strategy in the future.

A successful recruitment strategy starts with an understanding of the organization's talent requirements. This is a phase that requires attention and time because it serves as the foundation, for all future talent acquisition efforts. Neglecting this process or rushing through it can lead to inefficiencies. Worse, hiring candidates who are not suitable.

Identifying Available Positions
The first step in this journey is to pinpoint the future job openings within the organization. It goes beyond listing the open positions; it involves closely examining the company's strategic plans, growth projections, and potential areas where teams should expand or new roles may be created. Accurately

forecasting for the next 12 to 18 months in alignment with the company's objectives and growth expectations becomes crucial.

When documenting these roles it is important to include:
- The job title, department, and location of each position
- How this role fits into the broader team structure
- The objectives and responsibilities associated with the position
- Day-to-day tasks and operational requirements
- Required skills and tools
- Abilities and communication skills needed
- Any pressing reasons that require hiring

This comprehensive breakdown goes beyond concepts (like "we need more data science engineers") and provides a list of roles and their corresponding requirements.

Identifying Required Skills
Once we have outlined the roles, the next step is to identify the skills and attributes necessary for success in these positions. This identification process should include a combination of expertise as well as intangible qualities like mindset, behaviour, and intellectual capacity. Some categories to consider are

- Functional expertise, which includes skills, knowledge, and experience levels
- Cognitive abilities that encompass aspects like adaptability in learning, problem-solving capabilities, and decision-making skills
- Leadership and collaborative skills that focus on the ability to influence others to work effectively within teams and communicates well across teams

- Effectiveness traits such as taking initiative, time management abilities, and resilience when facing pressure
- Motivation and cultural fit to ensure alignment with the organizations core values and a genuine passion for its mission

During this phase, hiring managers play a crucial role in distinguishing between the mandatory competencies versus desirable ones that are not essential to create target candidate profiles.

Once you have gathered all the details about the role and identified the competencies, the next step is to consolidate this information into target candidate profiles. These profiles serve as outlines of the candidates and should include:

- Details about their educational background, including years of experience and relevant areas of study
- A breakdown of their previous work experience highlighting the companies they've worked for
- Specific hard skills such as expertise, proficiency with tools and specialized knowledge
- Soft skills like collaboration, effective communication and problem-solving abilities
- Attributes that align with company values and mission to ensure a fit
- Factors that motivate them such as opportunities for career growth desire for challenges or preference for autonomy.

These profiles strike a balance between requirements and desirable attributes. While it may be challenging to find a candidate who perfectly matches all criteria, having a profile helps guide the sourcing and evaluation process.

Researching Market Dynamics

An overlooked aspect of this work is researching the external talent market and staying informed about industry trends. This research should cover:

- Hiring trends among competitors: understanding where they are focusing their efforts and how urgently they are hiring
- Salary benchmarks to ensure that competitive compensation packages are offered
- Talent availability: important skill sets in demand or limited supply
- Considering location factors, to identify talent hubs

The research offers insights into the talent market helping us understand the challenges and opportunities that may arise in the future. This knowledge allows us to create a strategic approach to sourcing talent.

Utilizing Data-Driven Strategies

To develop a talent strategy, it is crucial to rely on data-driven approaches. However, it is essential to analyze and identify the relevant and predictive metrics within the available data. For instance, a high turnover rate in one location might not indicate an issue, that could be an isolated incident. Similarly, a role that attracts a large number of applicants does not automatically guarantee the quality of these candidates. Instead, we should focus on metrics that genuinely reflect success and use them as the foundation for our sourcing strategy.

Differentiating between data and relevant information is of utmost importance. Concentrating on metrics that accurately represent candidate success across locations and over time is vital for creating effective sourcing campaigns.

The initial stage of understanding talent needs plays a role in developing a sourcing plan. This stage involves steps; identifying current and upcoming roles and outlining the necessary competencies and attributes. Then it's important to create comprehensive candidate profiles and research the market dynamics.

When implemented with meticulousness and accuracy, this phase establishes a groundwork for recruitment endeavors. It guarantees the hiring procedure is effective and in harmony with the culture and long-term aspirations of the organization. The objective is to allure and recruit individuals who are not just competent, but also align well with the overall goals and mission of the company.

MASTER THE ART OF SOURCING

When it comes to talent acquisition, clearly defining your talent needs is the starting point. The real challenge lies in mastering the sourcing techniques which offer opportunities for innovation. This process can be compared to an art form that demands creativity, precision, and a deep understanding of today's recruitment landscape.

Embracing Advanced Technological Tools

One crucial aspect of this art form is embracing the power of technology. Using AI-enabled tools and advanced software in sourcing is incredibly important. Platforms like *Connectifier* (acquired by LinkedIn in February 2016) and *Entelo* utilize intelligence to efficiently analyze data, helping identify suitable candidates that meet specific requirements. These tools are invaluable in navigating through profiles.

Now let's look at the programmatic job advertising platforms like *Joveo*, *Appcast*, or *Radancy*. These platforms revolutionized how companies reach potential candidates by dynamic targeting, ensuring that job ads reach the most suitable candidates based on their online behavior and preferences. Moreover, automated campaigns for nurturing and outreach can effectively handle high-volume candidate communications while maintaining engagement without burdening the recruitment team's resources.

Harnessing the Power of Networks
Leveraging networks remains an important aspect of sourcing strategies. It involves tapping into both personal and professional networks to spread the word about open positions.

Encouraging employees to recommend candidates not only brings in hires who align with our company culture but also boosts team morale by involving them in our overall growth.

Referral programs with incentives are an effective way to encourage this behavior. However, it's important to expand our networking approach beyond the internal teams. Hosting events that bring together a range of individuals, including staff, alumni, vendors, and community members helps us to create a network of connections and potential candidates.

Additionally, establishing ambassador programs empowers employees to act as brand representatives and share job openings within their networks. These initiatives effectively transform every employee into a recruiter, expanding our reach in the talent market.

Building and Promoting a Strong Employer Brand
An overlooked aspect of talent acquisition is employer branding. How we present ourselves as a company greatly influences our ability to attract top-notch talent. It goes beyond having an appealing careers page or crafted job descriptions; it's all about genuinely communicating our culture, values, and vision at every touchpoint with the candidates.

Providing a positive experience throughout the application process and interviews plays a crucial role in reinforcing our employer brand. Streamlining these processes to be engaging, respectful, and reflective of the company's culture not only attracts candidates but also leaves a lasting positive impression regardless of the outcome.

Collecting and acting upon feedback is also crucial in this process. Using platforms like *Glassdoor* to gather feedback and make improvements based on those inputs, shows a dedication to constantly improving and respecting the candidate experience.

Moving Beyond Conventional Job Boards
Going beyond job boards is necessary because they mainly attract active job seekers. A significant portion of the talent pool consists of those candidates – who are not actively searching

for a job but are open to opportunities. To reach these passive candidates, we need to think outside the box.

This involves developing targeted strategies to engage with candidates. It includes exploring community groups, professional associations, and networking events where these individuals are likely to be present. Engaging with trade publications and online forums can also help us connect with candidates. This approach requires persistence and creativity as we strive to establish a presence in spaces where potential candidates naturally gather.

Adopting a Continuous Prospecting Mindset
Adopting a mindset of continuous prospecting is key to mastering the art of sourcing. This means not only engaging with candidates just during active recruitment periods, it involves building and maintaining relationships with talent within the industry over time.

You can develop a strong network by engaging with candidates on professional platforms offering mentorship, and staying connected with past applicants. This network becomes an asset as it creates a pool of individuals that can be tapped into as needs arise. Therefore someone you connect with casually today could turn out to be the candidate tomorrow.

Moreover, this ongoing engagement approach helps you understand the evolving needs and aspirations of candidates. This understanding allows effective communication when the right opportunity arises.

Mastering the art of sourcing is an endeavor that combines technology with genuine human connections. It involves building an employer brand and going beyond job boards to reach passive candidates who may not actively seeking new opportunities. Importantly, it requires adopting a mindset of engagement with the talent market.

By implementing these strategies, organizations can ensure a stream of candidates who not only possess the necessary technical skills but also align well with the company's culture and long-term objectives. This holistic approach to sourcing is what sets apart successful recruitment strategies in the competitive landscape of talent acquisition.

GO ON THE OFFENSE

In the world of recruitment, successful recruiters take a proactive approach rather than being passive. They go the mile that others don't. This means delving into data, unleashing their creativity, and reaching out to candidates even before they start thinking about making a change – essentially keeps them one step ahead of the competition.

Focusing on Candidates Who Aren't Actively Looking
A portion of the talent market consists of candidates – those who aren't actively searching for new opportunities but would consider a great offer. These individuals may include professionals currently employed but open to possibilities, freelancers who are content with their independence, and individuals engaged in academic pursuits. Making up to 70% of the candidate pool, these passive prospects often possess skills

and are highly desired by recruiters – sometimes referred to as the *"purple squirrels"* in the talent industry. However, these candidates usually won't approach you; instead, you need to engage them through planned sourcing campaigns that catch their attention.

Discovering Promising Talent Pools
Identifying your candidates and locating them effectively requires analysis and research. This can involve mining data, from CRM systems as well as external databases to find standout individuals across various fields – from customer service experts to top-performing sales professionals.

To find thinkers and innovators it's worth exploring publications, patents, and lists of conference speakers. Tools like *Crystal Knows* and *LinkedIn Recruiter* can be incredibly helpful in this search as they can assist in pinpointing individuals with the desired backgrounds, skills, and networks.

Executing Direct Outreach
When it comes to reaching out to candidates, a direct and targeted approach is essential. This can involve customized email campaigns like *LinkedIn InMails*, personalized social media messages, and even cold calls. Consistent communication through channels is crucial to keep your brand and opportunities at the forefront of candidates' minds. The messaging should emphasize the value and career growth potential you offer. It's important to think broadly; for example, someone currently working as a marketing manager might become a head of sales. While outbound campaigns require effort, the return

on investment can be substantial, bringing in high-quality candidates who might not have been reached otherwise.

Building Foundations with Emerging Talent

Another effective strategy is to establish connections with emerging talents who are early in their careers. This can be achieved through partnerships with institutions, training programs, boot camps, or community organizations. By offering internships and apprenticeships, you not only enhance your reputation among entrants into the workforce but also strengthen your capabilities as an organization.

By fostering these relationships even when you're not actively hiring, you create a sort of "talent pipeline" that can provide a steady stream of qualified candidates in the future. This approach aligns with the wisdom shared by Warren Buffet; *"Someone's sitting in the shade today because someone planted a tree a long time ago."*

Integrating Candidate Conversations into Daily Activities

Incorporating conversations with candidates should be an essential part of a recruiter's everyday routine, rather than just something done when there's an immediate need to hire. Setting goals for outreach every week can help maintain this practice. Allocate time not only for reaching out to new prospects but also for nurturing existing connections. Even short conversations can help establish rapport and gain insights, enabling you to stay connected with individuals over time. When there is a need to hire you will already have an established network to tap into. Successful proactive recruitment requires a combination of discipline and creativity.

Transforming recruitment into a process involves several key strategies. It entails targeting candidates through campaigns, identifying potential talent pools through thorough research, engaging in direct outreach efforts, building solid relationships with emerging talent, and integrating candidate conversations seamlessly into daily routines.

By implementing these methods recruiters can establish the organization as a place for individuals to seek employment. Additionally, it guarantees a pool of candidates who can be readily considered when the need arises. By adopting these strategies, recruiters can effectively build a robust talent pipeline that serves both immediate and long-term hiring goals, ultimately contributing to the organization's success and growth.

As we near the end of this chapter, let's take a moment to revisit and delve deeper into the journey of Eva and her team at Accel Technologies.

Eva's first crucial step was realizing that Accel's current recruitment methods were inadequate. Their approach had been lacking structure, which is a common pitfall for many growing companies. The decision to transition to a strategic sourcing plan went beyond adopting new techniques; it represented a fundamental shift in mindset from passive recruitment to actively seeking out talented individuals.

Creating an In-Depth Candidate Profile

Eva's collaboration with department heads played a role in this process. By predicting job openings and identifying the skills they developed comprehensive candidate profiles.

These profiles went beyond job descriptions by incorporating elements of Accel's work culture and environment. This holistic approach was crucial in identifying candidates who would not only excel in their roles but thrive within the organization as a whole.

Refining the Sourcing Strategy
The decision to focus on targeted sourcing channels such as *GitHub* and *Stack Overflow* proved to be a game changer for Eva's team. Rather than waiting for potential candidates to come to Accel, they proactively sought out talent where it was most abundant. This shift allowed them to tap into a wealth of individuals who aligned perfectly with their requirements.

This proactive approach significantly expanded their pool of hires.

Introducing Structured Interviews
Eva introduced interviews with purposes in mind. Firstly they ensured that the evaluation of candidates was consistent and thorough. By training interviewers to ask planned behavioral questions, Eva made sure that the team could accurately assess not only the candidate's technical skills, but also their soft skills such as teamwork, problem-solving, and adaptability.

Addressing Challenges and Overcoming Bias
Eva's team encountered a challenge related to biases in the hiring process. To overcome this, they incorporated perspectives into the interview and selection process. This approach not only enriches the evaluation process but also promotes fairness and inclusivity in making hiring decisions.

Quantifying Assessment Data
Another significant improvement was transitioning from intuition-based to evidence-based hiring decisions. By quantifying candidate assessment data, the team could make justifiable choices when it came to hiring. This data-driven approach also enabled tracking and analysis of the hiring process for continuous improvement.

Continuous Improvement and Feedback
Eva recognized that talent acquisition is an evolving process. By implementing feedback loops and consistently analyzing recruitment data, her team could refine their strategies, making them more effective over time. This adaptability was key to their success in a dynamic and competitive tech industry.

The Influence
These changes had an impact, and that was profound. The strategic recruitment of 25 top-notch professionals in two quarters was evidence of the effectiveness of their approach. These individuals weren't just placeholders for the open positions; they were highly skilled experts who brought immense value to both their teams and the entire company. The discovery of talent referred to as "*purple squirrels*" just not only showcased the success of their strategies but also demonstrated their dedication to finding the perfect match for both the role and company culture.

Expanding Beyond Hiring
Eva's vision extended beyond filling job vacancies. She aimed to establish a recruitment system that would support Accel's long-term growth. This involved not just hiring the people, but also focusing on integrating them into the company and

developing their skills. Ensuring that new hires were effectively onboarded and aligned with Accel's objectives and values was crucial for their success.

Looking Forward

As Accel achieved its hiring goals and entered its phase of growth, Eva recognized that this was not the end of the journey. The field of talent acquisition is ever-evolving and presents challenges and opportunities every day.

Eva and her team were fully dedicated to maintaining their advantage in the fast-paced world of tech talent acquisition. They believed in learning, staying ahead of the curve, and adapting their strategies accordingly.

Important Lessons

Eva's experience at Accel Technologies offers insights for any organization seeking to revitalize its talent acquisition approach. The key lessons learned from their journey include the significance of a proactive recruitment strategy, the value of structured interview processes, the necessity of data-driven decision-making, and the importance of continuously improving recruitment methods.

Eva's leadership brought a shift at Accel Technologies that went beyond merely filling positions efficiently. This shift was instrumental in enabling scaling up while ensuring long-term sustainability. As we conclude this chapter, it becomes evident that strategic talent acquisition is a dynamic process that demands vigilance, innovation, and adaptation to outpace competitors in the ever-evolving talent landscape.

CHAPTER 2
ASSESSING BEYOND THE RESUME

INTERVIEWING FOR INSIGHTS

As a hiring manager at a growing tech company, Sana faced the challenge of finding a person for an engineering management position. The success of her team and the entire company relied on this decision. With determination, she started the process of how significant this hire would be.

After a search, Sana had a pool of promising candidates at her disposal. Among them one resume stood out; Nate's. His credentials were an engineering degree from a university, leadership experience at a well-known startup, and strong technical expertise. On paper, Nate appeared to be the fit for the role Sana needed to fill.

During Nate's interview, he solidified his position as the candidate. He confidently answered questions and demonstrated quick thinking ability. His responses to leadership inquiries were equally impressive, reflecting his self-assured demeanor. Sana could feel that Nate's impressive resume truly came to life during the interview. She was almost convinced that he was the choice and ready to extend an offer.

However, Raj, one of Sana's colleagues had some reservations. While Raj recognized Nate's background and polished performance during the interview, he had a sense that there might be more to discover beneath the surface. Raj had doubts about whether Nate's smooth responses were hiding any weaknesses. Additionally, he expressed concerns about how Nate would fit into their well-knit team.

Considering Raj's concerns, Sana agreed to explore Nate's suitability for the position. They designed a case study specifically tailored to simulate the real-world challenges associated with the role. This would not only test Nate's abilities but also evaluate his problem-solving skills and adaptability.

During this assessment, some flaws became apparent in what seemed like Nate's demeanor. Although his technical skills were above average, they didn't align with the level of expertise he claimed to possess. Moreover, when confronted with scenarios involving conflict resolution, Nate seemed flustered. He struggled to provide examples of successfully managing such situations.

The next step involved reaching out to Nate's references. Sana and Raj contacted his manager who was polite but subtly hinted at collaboration issues during Nate's role. This feedback portrayed an image of Nate compared to what was indicated in his resume and initial interview.

To gain an understanding of Nate's suitability for the position, Sana opted to have one meeting with him focusing on how well he would fit into the company culture. She delved into his reasons for wanting to leave his job. She tried to explore his values. During their conversation, Nate became more open and candid. He admitted to facing challenges in getting support for his ideas at his job. Confessed that he sometimes lacked patience when mentoring junior engineers.

This last interaction provided Sana with clarity. Although Nate seemed impressive on paper and possessed strengths, he lacked the qualities necessary for success in the role they were trying to fill. It became evident that a comprehensive assessment process involving tests, reference checks, and in-depth discussions about values and team dynamics were crucial for evaluating a candidate's compatibility.

With this realization, Sana decided not to hire Nate. She continued her search and soon came across Gwen. While Gwen's resume may not have initially stood out like Nate's, she emerged as the candidate through an evaluation process. Gwen not only showcased expertise but also demonstrated an exceptional ability to mentor team members while aligning with the company culture.

The impact of hiring Gwen was immediate and positive. She quickly demonstrated her value by excelling in her position and making contributions to the team. This experience taught Sana a lesson. She realized that resumes provide a perspective on a candidate's abilities and suitability. To truly assess a candidate's suitability, it is crucial to dig and evaluate their skills, motivations, and those essential soft skills that often separate a candidate from an exceptional one. Ultimately it was an evaluation approach that revealed the candidate for the role

– someone who not only looked impressive on paper but also proved their worth in practice.

Employing a Structured Yet Flexible Interviewing Method
A candidate's resume, which provides an overview of their journey only gives us a glimpse into their potential. To truly understand a candidate's abilities, and motivations, and fit within our organization's culture, we should rely heavily on the interviewing process. This process goes beyond a formality; it is a tool, in our talent acquisition toolkit. It requires an approach that effectively uncovers a candidate's experiences and skills to ensure a thorough and accurate assessment.

One crucial aspect of the interviewing process is establishing an adaptable methodology. This means creating a framework with questions to ensure fairness across all interviews. However, it's equally important to maintain a flow that allows for dialogue. Striking this balance helps us gather information in a way and provides us with an understanding of the candidate's capabilities and personality.

We make it a point to document insights after each interview while they are still fresh in our minds. Additionally, we should grade candidates based on predefined criteria to standardize the evaluation process and enable comparisons between applicants. This structured approach forms the foundation for making well-informed hiring decisions.

Crafting Relevant Questions for Evaluating Core Competencies
The essence of conducting interviews lies in formulating questions that directly correspond to the skills and abilities

required for the role. These questions should prompt candidates to provide examples from their experiences, especially those that highlight important qualities such as problem-solving, teamwork, and attention to detail. It's not sufficient to hear about these experiences; delving deeper with follow-up questions can unveil the candidate's thought processes, decision-making strategies, and how they assess factors in real-world situations. This thorough exploration offers insights into their performance on the job.

Evaluating Cultural Fit
It is significant to evaluate how well a candidate aligns with an organization's culture, values, and work style. This evaluation can be accomplished by designing situational questions. The goal is to determine whether a candidate's preferred work environment, motivators, and demonstrated traits like empathy and ethical judgment, resonate with the organization's ethos. It is crucial to move beyond likability and focus on attitudes, motivations, and behaviors that harmonize with the company culture.

Navigating Challenging Conversations
During an interview it is important not to shy from discussing the difficult aspects of a candidate's career journey. Engaging in conversations about career gaps, terminations, acknowledged weaknesses, or past mistakes can be enlightening for both parties involved.

The way a candidate discusses these topics can tell us a lot about their self-awareness, accountability, resilience, and capacity for learning and growth. These conversations require sensitivity and tact. They often give us insights into a candidate's character and potential for development.

Practicing Active Listening
One of the often overlooked skills in interviews is the ability to listen actively. Approaching an interview as a conversation rather than treating it like an interrogation, can completely change the dynamic. Creating an environment where candidates feel comfortable expressing themselves openly, involves encouraging body language, being attentive, and avoiding interruptions.

Active listening means more than understanding what is being said; it means picking up on cues that show a candidate's level of engagement, humility, empathy, and overall demeanor. This approach does not put candidates at ease. It encourages them to be their authentic selves allowing us to get a better understanding of how well they would fit within our organization.

The interview process is a stage, in our journey to find champions. It requires both structure and flexibility, thoughtful questioning, assessing fit, having the courage to address topics head-on, and actively practicing good listening skills.

Gaining expertise in the art of conducting interviews gives us an understanding of candidates. It goes beyond what's written on their resume, allowing us to discover their abilities and compatibility with the role and the organization.

TESTING FOR SUCCESS

While interviews and resumes play a role in evaluating a candidate's suitability for a position, they only provide a view. To gain an understanding of a candidate's abilities, it is vital to incorporate skills tests and assessments into the hiring process. These tools offer data on aspects of a candidate's profile including technical skills, cognitive abilities, personality traits, and motivations. Designed assessments can reveal insights that might otherwise be missed in interviews alone.

Evaluating Technical and Functional Expertise

For roles that require functional knowledge, practical tests and simulations are invaluable. These assessments should be customized to reflect the real-life challenges and tools relevant to the job. For example, candidates applying for an engineering position may be given a coding project that simulates real-world scenarios they would encounter in their role. Similarly, sales positions could involve role-playing exercises where candidates demonstrate product pitching or engage in simulated customer conversations. The key is to develop tests that not only evaluate skills but also measure the ability to apply those skills in practical situations. The quality and effectiveness of their outputs serve as indicators of proficiency.

Assessing Cognitive Abilities

Understanding a candidate's capabilities is another aspect of the assessment process.

This can be done through the use of tools such as aptitude tests, IQ tests, Watson-Glaser Critical Thinking Appraisal (WGCTA), etc. These tests can provide insights into cognitive abilities, including problem-solving skills adaptability to new challenges, attention to detail, and quantitative reasoning capabilities. By using these assessments we can gather data on a candidate's sharpness and make informed predictions about their ability to process information, make decisions wisely and quickly adjust to new situations.

Assessing Personality Fit
Understanding how a candidate's personality aligns with the requirements of the role and the organization's culture is crucial. Validated measures such as *Myers Briggs Type Indicator* (MBTI), DISC assessments, or *Hogan Personality Inventory*, can offer insights into a candidate's personality traits. Factors like extroversion versus introversion, patience levels, resilience, attention to detail, and teamwork are some major considerations. These traits have an impact on how candidates interact with others in the environment and manage stress.

Discovering Candidate Motivations
A candidate's motivations and values play a role in their behavior at work and overall job satisfaction. Tools like Values Inventories or Motives Values and Preferences Inventory provide information, about what drives candidates in their lives.

Different individuals can have varying levels of need for achievement, power, affiliation, and security. By understanding these motivations, we can better predict how a candidate will perform in environments and whether they align with our organization's values and goals.

It's important to remember that there is no one-size-fits-all approach when it comes to assessments. Each role may require a set of skills and competencies, so we should choose assessments accordingly. It's crucial to select tools that offer valid insights into the abilities and traits needed for the role. Equally important is avoiding assessments that lack validity or introduce bias into the hiring process. By integrating these tools into our evaluation process, we can significantly improve the depth and accuracy of candidate assessments.

Incorporating assessments into our hiring process allows us to gain an objective and comprehensive view of a candidate's potential. By combining insights from interviews with data obtained through skills tests and personality assessments, we can make more informed decisions based on evidence. This approach not only increases the accuracy of talent acquisition but also helps build a workforce that possesses the necessary skills while aligning with our organizational culture and values.

AVOIDING BIAS AND GAPS

In the realm of talent acquisition, seasoned recruiters can have blind spots, biases, and gaps in their evaluation processes. Without a structured approach, these biases can result in overlooking qualities in candidates or unintentionally favoring certain individuals. It is vital to develop a methodology that minimizes bias and offers an understanding of each candidate to ensure effective hiring practices.

Establishing Objective Evaluation Criteria

The initial step towards creating a recruitment process is to define consistent criteria for assessing candidates. This helps mitigate the risks associated with instinctual decision-making, which can lead to biased outcomes. One practical approach is developing an assessment scorecard that takes into account factors, such as

- Skills and experience - Ratings based on the candidate's proficiency in required competencies
- Interview performance - Evaluation of the candidate's communication skills, engagement level, and overall demeanor during interviews
- Assessment results - Scores obtained from tests, personality inventories, or other relevant evaluations
- References - Considering feedback from employers or colleagues regarding the candidate's performance and work ethic
- Cultural fit - Assessing how the candidate aligns, with the organizations core values and motivators

By implementing these evaluation criteria, recruiters can strive for assessments that minimize biases and provide a more holistic view of each candidate. To ensure fairness and make comparisons, it is crucial to evaluate all candidates based on a set of criteria. It is also important to document impressions and evaluations, after each interaction with a candidate to ensure that assessments are accurate.

Incorporating Diverse Perspectives in Evaluations

To reduce biases, one effective strategy is to involve a panel of evaluators in the candidate assessment process. By including individuals from various departments and different backgrounds, the panel can bring diversity and minimize the chances of overlooking important aspects. It is essential for panel members to independently evaluate candidates before engaging in group discussions to prevent groupthink. This approach encourages a rounded perspective on each candidate reducing the influence of any viewpoint.

Concentrating on Performance Indicators
When evaluating candidates, it is important to focus on performance indicators that have proven to be predictors of success. Factors such as learning ability, problem-solving skills, achievement orientation, and emotional intelligence, are indicators of superficial attributes like prestigious alma maters or personal charm. Evaluators should be encouraged to question assumptions about backgrounds or experiences indicating competency, instead rely on evidence-based factors linked to job performance.

Valuing Real Accomplishments Over Prestigious Backgrounds
It's important not to overvalue backgrounds or experiences, with well-known companies when assessing candidates. Instead, real accomplishments should be given weight in the evaluation process. It is important to prioritize the substance of a candidate's accomplishments and the impact of their work. This approach requires delving into the candidate's background to understand the actual results they have achieved rather than being influenced solely by the reputation of the institutions or companies they have been associated with. Shifting from a focus on pedigree to a performance-based assessment helps identify candidates who have demonstrated the skills and qualities for success in the role.

Conducting Regular Audits of Hiring Practices
Regular auditing of the hiring practices is crucial for identifying any biases or gaps. This involves analyzing hiring decisions, evaluating the effectiveness of recruitment channels, and assessing how candidates from different demographic backgrounds fare throughout the hiring process. If certain groups consistently face challenges or are underrepresented in the recruitment pipeline, it is important to investigate and address these issues. Conducting audits and making adjustments to improve fairness, inclusivity, and effectiveness are essential.

To summarize, developing a recruitment process that minimizes bias while providing an understanding of each candidate requires key strategies. These include establishing evaluation criteria, involving a group of evaluators focusing on evidence-based performance indicators, valuing achievements over pedigrees or prestige, and conducting regular audits to ensure ongoing improvement, in fairness, inclusivity, and effectiveness.

By adopting these approaches companies can enhance their hiring decisions by being better informed, fairer, and more impactful.

As we wrap up this exploration of the multifaceted realm of talent acquisition, it's crucial to reflect on how each aspect of the process contributes to the objective of identifying and securing top-notch talent. By revisiting Sana's journey and her company's successful hiring of Gwen, we can observe how the implementation of these strategies leads to talent acquisition.

The Importance of a Strategic Approach
Sana's story serves as an example highlighting the risk involved in relying on a resume. However, her decision to explore beyond that document and consider a wider range of candidates ultimately led her to Gwen, whose skills and attributes were better aligned with the company's requirements.

Interviewing for Comprehensive Insights
Moving on to discussing interviewing strategies, we underscored the importance of competency-based interviews that provide a view of each candidate. Sana's experience with Nate exemplifies this notion as she witnessed his interview performance, but later discovered his struggles during in-depth assessments, which shed light on the limitations posed by conventional interviews. Through a thoughtful interview process, Sana was able to uncover the abilities and suitability of Gwen for the role.

Ensuring Genuine Competence
Including assessments of skills and personality tests in the hiring process played a role. These assessments provided data that complemented the aspects of interviews. Sana's experience highlighted this when she put Nate's interpersonal skills to the test revealing areas where he had gaps that were not evident from his resume or initial interviews.

Addressing Bias for Fair Evaluation
We also discussed the topic of minimizing bias in recruitment. Sana initially leaned towards Nate due to his professional background, which is an example of unconscious bias. However, by implementing evaluations and seeking perspectives, Sana was able to overcome these biases and identify Gwen as the

candidate whose skills and values truly aligned with the company's needs.

Integrating Strategies for Comprehensive Assessment
By combining these strategies in her hiring processes, Sana successfully appointed Gwen. Although Gwen's resume may not have initially stood out like Nate's, her true potential was revealed through an evaluation that included interviews, skill assessments, and a focus on cultural fit. This outcome highlights the importance of taking a thoughtful approach to talent acquisition.

Lessons, moving forward...
Sana's experience provides insights for recruiters and hiring managers. Firstly, it is crucial to have a sourcing plan in place to identify a pool of potential candidates. Secondly, the interview process should be well structured, yet flexible enough for an understanding of each candidate's skills and suitability. Thirdly, incorporating skill and personality assessments into the hiring process can provide insights. Lastly, actively working to reduce bias ensures an equitable evaluation process.

Talent acquisition requires a scientific approach that combines strategy, structure, and understanding. Each stage of the process from sourcing to selection, plays a role in building a team that not only meets the technical requirements but also enhances the organization's culture and values. As seen in Sana's case, thoughtful and comprehensive hiring practices can uncover talents like Gwen who align with both the role and organizational values, leading to success.

CHAPTER 3
MAKING DATA-DRIVEN DECISIONS

QUANTIFYING CANDIDATE ASSESSMENT

Zeero Technologies, a growing tech company, was evolving. Ronnie, the hiring manager for the sales team, faced a crucial decision. He had been given the task of doubling the number of sales team members within months. This meant he had to act to secure talents, while also ensuring that these new hires would be a good fit for the company. The stakes were high. Finding the balance between speed and accuracy in recruitment was essential.

Traditionally Zeero's sales department relied heavily on intuition and gut feelings when making hiring decisions. This approach was endorsed by Ronnie's boss, Merlyn. She valued qualities like passion and professionalism more than qualifications or data-driven assessments. However, this approach had its downsides. It sometimes resulted in employees who didn't align well with the company culture, and missed sales targets. After witnessing these challenges, Ronnie felt compelled to transition towards a strategic and data-driven approach to recruitment.

Ronnie embarked on creating an organized evaluation scorecard as a solution. This tool aimed to provide an assessment of each candidate by incorporating evaluation results from sources such as interviews focusing on key competencies and alignment, with the company's core values.

Working closely with the HR department, he implemented sales simulations to objectively evaluate candidates' negotiation skills, ability to handle objections, and presentation capabilities. Moreover, candidates were required to complete personality and motivational assessments, which provided insights, into their suitability for the team.

Armed with this data, Ronnie initiated the selection process. His focus was on candidates who exhibited revenue-generating abilities, persistence, and a willingness to mentor their colleagues – qualities that he had identified in the company's performers. This approach led him to prioritize candidates with proven track records over those who merely excelled in interviews. Ronnie's strategy aimed not at filling positions but at ensuring that each new hire would make a significant contribution to the team's success.

Initially skeptical about dedicating time to evaluations due to the urgent need for new hires, Merlyn soon witnessed the undeniable results. The individuals recruited by Ronnie showcased selling skills and a strong work ethic right from the start. Issues related to fit that had previously hindered team cohesion and performance were noticeably absent.

In a matter of months, Ronnie's team surpassed their sales targets while fostering a collaborative environment. His choice to resist the pressure of rushing into hiring decisions and instead prioritize an evidence-based recruitment process was proving to be a success.

After witnessing the impact of Ronnie's approach, Merlyn became a believer in the data-driven methodology. Together they began revamping the hiring processes throughout Zeero Technologies aiming to reduce reliance on intuition and gut instincts. This shift towards fact-based recruitment practices was quickly adopted company-wide, resulting in an enhancement in the quality of hires across all departments.

Six months later the revamped hiring strategy was yielding results. Positions were being filled efficiently with candidates who not only fit the immediate role but also proved to be long-term assets for the company. This caught the attention of investors and Wall Street analysts who commended Zeero for its transformation in talent management leading to an increase in the company's valuation.

Ronnie's unwavering commitment to a data-driven recruitment strategy had not reshaped the sales team. Had also triggered a fundamental shift in how Zeero Technologies approached acquiring talent.

This tale serves as evidence of how data can influence and guide decision-making in the competitive realm of recruitment.

In the field of talent acquisition, it is crucial to transform the process of evaluating candidates into a framework that allows for objective and fair hiring decisions. By implementing assessment tools, hiring teams can adopt a more data-driven approach to assessing candidates. This approach not only promotes objectivity during the hiring process but also ensures that decisions are based on the specific requirements of the position.

Creating Candidate Scorecards

The cornerstone of an assessment process is developing candidate scorecards. These scorecards are designed to evaluate candidates, across competencies, skills, and cultural alignment factors by using rating scales like 1 to 5. The criteria within these rubrics need to be clearly defined in terms of behavior and closely aligned with the role's requirements. Potential rating factors could include proficiency in areas like coding or financial modeling, thinking abilities in solving complex problems, management skills involving team leadership and strategic planning, as well as alignment with organizational cultural values such as collaboration, transparency, and innovation.

Assigning Weightage Based on Role Relevance

Assigning weightage to each evaluation criterion is an aspect of this process. The weighting should reflect the importance of each skill or competency toward achieving success in the role. For instance let's consider an accounting position where numerical accuracy is deemed crucial, than communication skills. In this case, numerical accuracy would be given more weight in the overall assessment score to prioritize the most critical competencies for that role.

Incorporating Empirical Assessment Data

To enhance the evaluation process, it is important to incorporate empirical assessment data into the scoring system.

This includes results from skills tests, cognitive assessments, and personality inventories. These assessments provide data to quantify capabilities such as attention to detail through error-checking tasks, cognitive reasoning abilities in processing complex information, sales acumen in objection handling and persuasive communication, and resilience in coping with setbacks and ambiguity.

Evaluating Interview Performance
In addition to tests and assessments, it is also important to evaluate candidates' performance during interviews using criteria. This can include assessing their level of engagement, clarity, relevance of their responses, communication style, and overall professionalism. It is crucial to focus on behaviors that reflect competencies rather than merely being influenced by a candidate's presentation skills or charisma.

Normalizing Scores Across Interview Panels
To ensure fairness and consistency in evaluations, it is necessary to compare and normalize scores across interview panels. This helps identify and address any biases or inconsistencies, among graders. For example, if an interviewer consistently rates candidates more than the rating given by the team, their ratings may need to be adjusted to align with the overall assessments of the broader team.

Analyzing Trends and Patterns
A thorough examination of scoring trends across skills and types of assessments can help identify any data points that may require further explanation. Additionally, identifying areas where candidates lack skills can provide valuable insights

for future training and development priorities within the organization. This analytical approach gives us information about both the group of candidates being evaluated and how effective our recruitment process is overall.

By converting evaluations into data, organizations can facilitate more objective comparisons between candidates based on facts. This structured approach to evaluating candidates promotes transparency in the hiring process. Using this data-driven methodology not only enhances the quality of hiring decisions, it also contributes to building a workforce that is well-suited for the job requirements and fits into the organizational culture.

Structured Decision-Making

In the fast-paced world of recruitment, shifting to a data-driven hiring process is essential. This requires adopting structured decision-making procedures. This approach aims to promote consistency across stages and eliminate personal biases that can influence the selection process. By following defined steps, clear guidelines, and involving all stakeholders, organizations can ensure that their hiring decisions are strategic and fair.

Establishing a Step-by-Step Hiring Protocol

Creating a defined and step-by-step decision-making flow is crucial for establishing a hiring process. This flow should outline roles and responsibilities at each stage to ensure a thorough evaluation of candidates. An example of such a process could include:

1. **Screening:** Recruiters conduct preliminary phone interviews to identify candidates who closely match the job requirements for further consideration.

2. **Hiring Manager Assessment:** The hiring manager conducts in-depth interviews based on competencies and reviews skills assessments to assess candidates' technical skills and functional abilities.

3. **Cross-Functional Panel Interviews:** Including evaluators from different departments in the panel brings perspectives into the assessment process enhancing the depth of candidate evaluation.

4. **Scorecard Rating:** The hiring manager uses an evaluation system to assess candidates taking into account factors such as their skills, performance in interviews, and suitability for the company's culture.

5. **Review and Decision by a Committee:** A committee carefully reviews all the gathered information, including assessment scores, interview notes, and feedback from evaluators. They utilize this data to decide who to hire.

6. **Extending an Offer:** The recruiter offers the job to the selected candidate with the condition that background and reference checks are completed satisfactorily.

Guidelines for Decision-Making Committees

When it comes to committees or panels involved in the hiring process, it is crucial to establish guidelines on which factors should be given priority during evaluations. It is important to train committee members to focus on criteria that are predictors of performance rather than personal preferences. Furthermore, ensuring a balanced representation of demographics within these committees can help minimize any biases.

Preventing Decisions Based on a Single Perspective
To avoid decisions influenced by one person's bias, it is essential to require consensus among stakeholders before extending job offers. Collecting assessments before engaging in group discussions can help prevent one evaluator from being influenced by another's perspective. Additionally granting HR or Legal departments veto power based on identified risks adds a layer of objectivity to the process.

Implementing 'Cool Off' Periods
Including 'Cool *Off*' periods at stages, such as after initial screenings, interviews, and before finalizing candidate selection, allows decision-makers to objectively reflect on data and assessments. These breaks help counteract biases or the influence of interactions leading to a more balanced and thoughtful decision-making process. However, these *'Cool Off'* periods should not be so lengthy that they allow candidates to pursue other job offers.

Maintaining Consistency and Diligence
It is crucial to maintain consistency and diligence by applying the level of scrutiny and following steps for every candidate, regardless of their background. Changing standards based on a candidate's affiliations with organizations introduces inconsistency and bias into the hiring process. Candidates from traditional backgrounds or lesser-known firms deserve

equal consideration and should undergo the same rigorous evaluation.

Auditing Hiring Outcomes
Regularly auditing hiring decisions is essential to ensure fairness and equity in the recruitment process. These audits should compare the demographics of selected candidates with the pool. If disparities are identified, such as certain demographic groups being chosen, it may indicate biases in criteria or the process itself. Continuous monitoring and adjustment of the hiring process are vital for maintaining fairness and inclusivity.

Implementing data-driven decision-making procedures in recruitment effectively reduces reliance on judgments. Organizations can enhance the advantages of assessments and data-driven evaluations by implementing discipline, objectivity, and accountability in their hiring decisions. This not only simplifies the recruitment process but also guarantees that candidates are selected based on their qualifications and suitability rather than subjective criteria.

Continuous Improvement
In the changing world of talent acquisition, it's important to recognize that hiring is not a one-time task. To achieve long-term success in recruitment, it's crucial to embrace a mindset of improvement. This means gathering data and feedback, analyzing recruitment processes, and making adjustments based on real-world experiences, analytical insights, and input from stakeholders.

Tracking Performance after Hiring

An element of improvement in recruitment is monitoring how new hires perform, adapt to their roles, and stay with the company over time. Gathering data on these metrics provides insights. Regular check-ins during the onboarding process are essential. Are hires meeting the expected ramp-up timelines? Are there any skill gaps? Reflecting on whether initial assessments predicted these outcomes can guide improvements in candidate evaluation and onboarding processes.

Seeking Feedback from New Hires and Managers

Gathering feedback from new team members at various stages - after 30, 60, and 90 days - of their onboarding can offer a candid view of the recruitment experience from the candidate's perspective. Understanding their challenges and suggestions for improvement can provide insights for refining the recruitment process.

Similarly, feedback from hiring managers regarding the performance of hires and the effectiveness of the recruitment process holds value. This continuous feedback loop guarantees that the process stays aligned with the requirements of both employees and managers.

Analyzing Recruitment Metrics

Analyzing recruitment metrics is crucial for identifying areas that require improvement. Metrics like the number of applications received per position, time taken to fill a vacancy, conversion rates from screening to interview, and acceptance rates for job offers can provide insights into patterns that indicate bottlenecks or inefficiencies in the process. Data-driven insights often play a role in uncovering issues within the recruitment workflow.

Closing the Feedback Loop

Integrating insights gathered from hire performance reviews, stakeholder feedback, and recruitment metrics back into the recruitment process is vital. This necessitates adjusting candidate assessment methods that may not align with job performance, refining evaluations to strike a balance between skills and cultural fit, and sharing successes to showcase effective practices.

Conducting Comprehensive Audits

Conducting audits of the recruitment process starting from sourcing candidates to onboarding them, ensures its continued effectiveness and relevance. This includes job descriptions, and assessment tools used at every interaction point throughout a candidate's journey through an inclusive lens to identify any potential biases. Comprehensive audits play a role in maintaining a recruitment process that's fair, efficient, and effective.

Improving Recruitment Strategies

Utilize the feedback and insights gained from audits to continuously refine your recruitment strategies. This may involve strengthening sourcing channels that consistently yield high-quality candidates or regularly revisiting role requirements to align with changing business priorities. While maintaining consistency in the recruitment process is important, it's equally vital to be adaptable and responsive to identified gaps and emerging needs.

Providing Ongoing Training for Recruitment Teams

As the recruitment process evolves, it's essential to ensure that the skills of your recruitment team are up to date. Implementing education programs like coaching clinics and recruiter boot camps can enhance their capabilities in areas such as data-driven assessment, mitigating bias, and optimizing the candidate experience. By investing in efforts your recruitment team will be equipped with the latest best practices in talent acquisition.

Nurturing a Culture of Continuous Improvement

Embedding a culture of improvement within the talent acquisition function can transform recruitment into a highly valuable capability. By translating insights into strategies and constantly seeking ways to improve the recruitment processes, organizations can reach heights of excellence in hiring. This not only enhances the quality of hires, also aligns the recruitment process, with evolving business needs and workforce dynamics.

In this chapter, we explored the complex processes involved in making data-driven decisions in selecting candidates strategically and continuously improving talent acquisition. These elements are essential for a recruitment strategy that not only ensures efficiency but also aligns with an organization's long-term objectives. To bring these concepts together, let's revisit Ronnie's story at Zeero Technologies—a narrative that demonstrates the impact of these approaches.

Data-Driven Decision Making; The Foundation of Modern Recruitment

The chapter began by highlighting the significance of data-driven decision-making in hiring practices. This approach encourages moving from relying on intuition and instead making decisions based on objective and measurable information. It involves integrating data points, such as skill assessments, cognitive tests, structured interviews, and cultural fit evaluations. By employing this method, hiring managers can objectively compare candidates. Select those who have the likelihood of succeeding in their roles.

Ronnie's experience at Zeero Technologies perfectly exemplified this concept. He recognized that while intuition and gut feelings had their merits, the rapid expansion of the sales team necessitated an approach supported by empirical data. By incorporating insights into the candidates' evaluation process, Ronnie significantly improved the quality of hires and made more informed decisions.

Structured Decision Making; Establishing Order and Fairness

We delved into the concept of decision-making, which plays a crucial role in ensuring fairness and consistency. This process involves implementing protocols and guidelines to maintain an approach to hiring. It includes defining stages in the recruitment process, seeking agreement among stakeholders, and employing structured scorecards for evaluating candidates.

In Ronnie's story, adopting a decision-making protocol proved to be a game changer. It allowed him to systematically assess each candidate while avoiding the risks associated with decisions. By requiring consensus from a group of stakeholders, he ensured that every candidate was evaluated from different perspectives, thereby minimizing individual biases.

Continuous Improvement; The Path Towards Recruitment Excellence

The aspect we discussed was the philosophy of continuous improvement. This approach recognizes that recruitment is an evolving process that benefits from evaluation and adjustments. By monitoring hire's performance, gathering feedback from newly hired individuals and their managers, analyzing recruitment metrics, and conducting periodic audits, organizations can refine their recruitment strategies over time.

Ronnie's commitment to improvement shone through his practice of tracking the performance of hired employees. He actively sought input, from both team members and managers, analyzed hiring metrics, and utilized these insights to further enhance his recruitment process.

Ronnie's Journey; A Story of Successful Talent Acquisition

As we wrap up this chapter, Ronnie's experience at Zeero Technologies serves as a testament to the effectiveness of these three elements in talent acquisition. His path from overcoming the challenge of expanding a sales team to successfully revolutionizing the company's hiring practices showcases the power of making data-driven decisions, implementing structured selection processes and maintaining a commitment to ongoing improvement.

The key to achieving talent acquisition in today's fast-paced business environment lies in seamlessly integrating data-driven decision-making, well-structured selection processes, and an unwavering dedication to ongoing improvement within the recruitment strategy.

Ronnie's success story at Zeero Technologies is an example of how these methods can revolutionize a company's recruitment process resulting in right hires, improved team performance, and ultimately significant business growth.

CHAPTER 4
SOURCING FOR SPECIALIZED ROLES

MAPPING UNIQUE CAPABILITIES

In the evolving world of technology and data science, securing top talent is crucial. Companies like Eager Analytics, a growing fintech firm, are on the verge of breakthroughs. They needed specialized talents in the fields like data engineering and machine learning. Maya, the head of talent acquisition at Eager Analytics, was well aware of this reality. However, finding skilled data scientists and machine learning experts has proven to be quite challenging due to the increasing demand in the industry.

Maya knew that the demand for niche skills in data and AI was expected to skyrocket by more than 50% in the next three years. The competition to attract these virtuosos was becoming fiercer by the day. Although Maya's team had initially tried sourcing candidates through channels like LinkedIn and general tech job boards, those efforts proved insufficient. The kind of talent Eager Analytics needed – individuals with skills in data science and machine learning – were not actively seeking opportunities or easily identifiable through conventional recruitment methods.

It became evident to Maya that a targeted and nuanced approach was necessary to attract these professionals. Her first step involved collaborating with her team to develop capability maps for data scientists and machine learning engineers. The maps provided information, about the technical skills, tool proficiencies, and problem-solving abilities that were crucial for these roles. This exercise highlighted the advanced nature of Eager's requirements, underscoring that common skill sets would not suffice for their ambitious projects.

With an understanding of the desired capabilities, Maya instructed her team to explore specialized channels. They immersed themselves in niche communities like *Slack* groups dedicated to data science, *subreddits* focused on machine learning and forums on platforms such as *Kaggle*. They also involved their engineers to help identify contributors on *GitHub*, because they recognized that impressive work often speaks louder than a traditional resume.

Furthermore, industry events, hackathons, and tech conferences became networking opportunities. These settings allowed access to the kind of talent they were searching for. Individuals who not only possessed skills but also had a genuine passion for their field.

Maya knew that attracting the attention of these sought-after professionals would require personalized approaches since many of them were not actively seeking new opportunities. She crafted narratives that highlighted the challenges and opportunities at Eager Analytics. Such as working with datasets engaging in groundbreaking machine-learning projects, and contributing to impactful products.

Her team highlighted how Eager prioritizes innovation and fosters an independent work environment. They also emphasized the opportunities to work with cutting-edge technologies. The goal was not to inform but to ignite enthusiasm in potential candidates about the prospects that awaited them at Eager.

The outcome of this shift in talent acquisition was impressive. Within months there was a 300% increase in applications from individuals specializing in next-generation data skills. Maya's approach which involved pinpointing the skills, required targeting channels frequented by these professionals and crafting messages that resonated with their aspirations proved to be highly effective.

Maya's success story at Eager Analytics provides a blueprint for sourcing talent in specialized domains. It underscores the significance of understanding the capabilities needed, engaging with candidates within their niche communities, and developing messaging that aligns with their career motivations and aspirations.

This chapter will explore the intricacies of sourcing for roles by drawing on Maya's experiences and delving into strategies that can be applied across industries. Whether it's fintech, healthcare, technology, or any other field where specialized skills are in demand—targeted sourcing techniques, compelling storytelling approaches, and strategic networking remain major factors for attracting top-tier talent.

When it comes to finding the talent for specialized positions, a one-size-fits-all approach is not sufficient. Achieving success in this field requires an examination of the skills and abilities necessary for each role. This process involves delving into technical expertise, competencies, motivators, and qualities that define success in these niche areas. By understanding these factors, recruiters can accurately evaluate candidates who not only possess the required skills but also have the potential to excel in their respective fields.

Analyzing Technical Proficiency
The initial step entails documenting the expertise that is crucial for excelling in specialized roles. This includes:

- Proficiency in skills like R, Python, or Tableau particularly for roles such as data scientists
- In-depth knowledge in areas such as statistical modeling, genomics or cloud architecture that play a significant role in specialized positions
- Familiarity with specific tools and technology stacks like *Spark*, *Kafka* or *Ansible* that are essential for certain technical roles
- Relevant experience with key platforms and systems along with a clear understanding of the minimum proficiency levels expected from prospective candidates

Standard technical qualifications serve merely as a starting point. What sets candidates apart is their niche abilities and expertise in areas that are at the forefront of their field.

Identifying Differentiating Competencies
In addition to the technical know-how, it is crucial to identify competencies that set candidates apart. These include:

- Cognitive strengths such as analytical reasoning, the ability to learn quickly, and skills in solving complex problems
- Soft skills like effective communication, creativity, and collaboration which are essential in almost every specialized role
- Knowledge creation skills that involve synthesizing new insights, innovating, and producing original research
- The ability to navigate situations and thrive in environments
- A strong inclination towards self-learning and expanding skills

These competencies are often the indicators of which candidates will not only adapt but also drive innovation and growth in fast-moving and evolving fields.

Understanding Candidate Motivations
Another crucial aspect is uncovering what motivates a talent. This could include:

- A desire to work with cutting-edge or emerging technologies
- A passion for making an impact on society through their work
- The aspiration to publish research and establish themselves as thought leaders
- The pursuit of career development opportunities and new challenges

People, in these fields often value having the freedom to work independently, flexibility in their schedules and the ability to think creatively. Understanding these motivations allows us to create persuasive messages that resonate with the candidates we want to attract.

Mapping the Candidate Journey
Analyzing the typical career paths and trajectories of talent in these specialized fields can provide further insights:

- Identifying common ways people enter the field, such as specific degree programs, companies, or initial roles
- Recognizing significant milestones like apprenticeships, notable publications, or experiences leading projects
- Understanding how people progress towards leadership or mastery positions
- Patterns of movement between fields and the potential for cross-disciplinary expertise

This understanding aids in sourcing talent that aligns with different career stages and in highlighting possible paths for advancement within the organization.

Researching Competitor Strategies
It is essential to research our competitors' strategies and benchmarks:

- Gaining an understanding of how competitors approach compensation, perks, and recognition for their employees
- Identifying methods used by competitors to attract and retain skilled individuals in niche areas
- Analyzing organizational models that empower performers within competitor companies
- Examining how competitors position their employer brand and build talent pipelines

This competitive intelligence is instrumental in developing counter-recruiting strategies and securing candidates that are highly sought after in the industry.

Effective sourcing for roles relies on capability mapping, which involves identifying the specific technical skills, soft competencies, motivators, and career development expectations desired by candidates. Moreover, gaining insights into how competitors attract and retain talent can greatly enhance recruitment strategies.

This meticulous approach to capability mapping goes beyond a recruitment tactic; it serves as a tool that drives sourcing excellence. It ensures that the recruitment process is not about filling positions but about finding individuals who possess a blend of skills, motivations, and potential that aligns with the organization's goals.

LEVERAGING SPECIALIZED CHANNELS

When it comes to filling roles relying on traditional recruitment methods like general job boards, often falls short. These roles demand a more innovative and targeted approach to sourcing, one that delves into channels where niche talent naturally congregates. By customizing the strategies, recruiters can effectively connect with candidates who are already excelling in their fields.

Exploring Niche Job Boards and Online Communities

A strategy is to explore niche job boards and online forums that cater specifically to the desired field. These specialized platforms tend to attract a skilled pool of candidates compared to general job sites. For example, platforms like *Dice* have gained recognition in the tech community, *MedReps* caters to medical sales professionals, and *ERE* serves as a hub for recruiters. Targeting these niche boards increases the chances of finding candidates who not only possess the required skills but are also actively involved in their profession.

Building Relationships with Associations and Networks
Professional associations and industry groups are some of the resources for identifying niche talent. By participating in these groups, attending their events, and engaging with members, recruiters can tap into a wealth of candidates. Establishing rapport with leaders and members of these associations can also lead to referrals, to a pool of qualified professionals. Alumni networks, particularly those connected to universities known for specific programs, can also be fruitful sources of talent.

Discovering Talent through Publications and Conferences
Publications, blogs, and conferences, are often frequented by top-notch professionals in fields. Identifying authors, speakers, or attendees who stand out for their expertise or innovative ideas can open doors to potential recruits. These individuals are typically recognized as leaders in their domains and their active participation in platforms reflects their proficiency and engagement in the field. Networking at conferences and seminars provides a chance to personally connect with these professionals, thereby increasing the likelihood of recruitment.

Leveraging Academic Collaborations

Building partnerships with institutions known for producing individuals in specific areas is another effective strategy. Engaging with students through lectures, collaborative projects or establishing connections with professors can grant access to emerging talent. Graduates from renowned programs often possess the latest skills and knowledge, making them prime targets for specialized roles.

Targeting Competitors High Performers

Researching individuals currently excelling in positions at rival or peer companies can lead to promising prospects. Ethically approaching standout performers, and highlighting the opportunities and challenges offered by your organization, can be a persuasive tactic. This approach ensures that the sourced candidates have already demonstrated their abilities within a context.

Encouraging Referrals

One effective way to enhance our sourcing efforts is by implementing a referral reward program. By offering incentives like cash bonuses, vacation days, gift cards, or charitable donations, we can motivate our current employees to recommend candidates from their networks. This approach transforms our workforce into a recruiting engine.

Spotting Rising Talent

To stay ahead of the game, it's important to keep an eye on industry media, publications, patents, and projects. Engaging with professionals at an early stage in their careers — before they gain attention — can give us a competitive edge in securing top emerging talent.

Harnessing Crowdsourcing for Prospecting

Another strategy is to connect with the contractors directly, or partner with staff augmentation service providers. Utilizing gig platforms like *UpWork* for sourcing independent contractors can come in handy at times. On the other hand, the staff augmentation service providers can give talents that are already handpicked and can start at the earliest possible time.

When it comes to sourcing for specialized roles, we need to break from traditional recruitment methods and adopt more creative and targeted approaches. Leveraging niche job boards, professional associations, industry publications, academic partnerships, competitor analysis, referral programs, and crowdsourcing allows recruiters to effectively connect with the high-caliber talent required for these positions. This proactive and multifaceted approach is crucial, in uncovering both hidden talent that meets the requirements of specialized roles.

CRAFTING COMPELLING PITCHES

In today's job market it takes more than a recruitment approach to attract niche talent. It requires creating compelling pitches that deeply resonate with the motivations and aspirations of these specialized professionals. Generic messaging about an employer brand just doesn't cut it when you're looking for individuals with sought-after skills and expertise. The process involves developing value propositions that directly address the prospects of career growth, meaningful work, and empowerment.

Shining a Light on Opportunities for Making a Difference

One strategy for attracting niche talent is to highlight the impact and societal contributions that their work can make.

The approach may vary depending on the field. For example, in non-profit sectors, emphasizing the potential to expand services and achieve life-changing results can be highly motivating. Climate scientists might be drawn to roles that offer opportunities for driving sustainability efforts. In fields like data science, emphasizing how data transparency plays a role in preventing fraud can be a factor. Meaningful work has a pull for talent who want to make a difference through their careers.

Prioritizing Career Growth and Development

Professionals in progressive fields place a high value on continuous learning and career advancement. It is crucial to articulate the opportunities your organization offers in terms of mentorship, training, and hands-on experiences. These opportunities can greatly enhance an individual's skills. Present your organization as a catalyst for unlocking their full potential, a place where they can grow and evolve professionally.

Communicating Culture and Values

When communicating your organization's culture and values during recruitment, it is essential to highlight whether your work environment aligns with the flexibility, autonomy, and inclusiveness that top niche talent seeks. Make it evident that candidates will have the chance to shape their roles and work on their terms. Remember that a cultural mismatch can significantly hinder the recruitment of talent.

Opportunities for Trailblazing

Motivated professionals often seek opportunities to drive innovation, conduct research, and be pioneers in their fields.

Describing how your organization supports trailblazing efforts and encourages innovation can be highly appealing to individuals.

Showcasing Resources and Support Systems
Additionally, it is important to showcase the resources and support systems available within your organization. While specialized talent tends to possess self-motivation and drive, emphasizing the resources provided by your organization further demonstrates its commitment, to supporting its employee's success.

Providing access to data sets, collaboration tools, mentorship, and learning budgets can give candidates confidence that they will have the resources and support to succeed.

Focusing on Solutions Rather Than Features
It's important to tailor your messaging towards the specific problems your customers face and the innovative products candidates will be working on. Specialized professionals are seeking purpose-driven work, rather than a list of job features or buzzwords.

Leveraging Peer Testimonials
Including testimonials from domain experts within your organization can add credibility to your pitches. When engineers share their experiences about the challenges and fulfillment they find in their work, it resonates effectively with fellow engineers. Peer testimonials provide a trustworthy perspective on the work and its impact.

Setting Realistic Expectations
Transparency about the challenges ahead and the time needed to master new complex systems is key. Top talents appreciate a clear understanding of what to expect, rather than being caught off guard later on. This openness establishes a foundation for a long-term productive relationship.

When it comes to recruiting for specialized roles, a one-size-fits-all approach to messaging simply doesn't work. Crafting targeted messages that effectively communicate the opportunities for career growth, autonomy, meaningful work, and cultural alignment is crucial. It's also important to allow technical colleagues to share their experiences and set expectations, about the role and its challenges. By tailoring your messaging to resonate with each function, you increase your chances of attracting top-tier talent that can help your organization thrive in its field.

As we wrap up this chapter, let's reflect on the journey of finding individuals, for specialized roles. It's a task that requires a mix of capability assessments, leveraging channels, and creating compelling pitches. This journey is exemplified by Maya's story, who's the head of talent acquisition at Eager Analytics. She faced challenges. She also celebrated triumphs while recruiting in niche domains.

Maya's Challenge; Finding Specialized Talent
Maya encountered a challenge when she had to find skilled data engineers and machine learning experts for a rapidly growing fintech company, Eager Analytics. The task became more complex due to the demand and limited availability of

such specialized talent. Maya initially tried methods and didn't have much success, which led her to adopt a more strategic approach.

Assessing Unique Abilities
Acknowledging the requirements of these roles, Maya took on the task of identifying the unique capabilities needed for these positions. This involved not only determining skills like proficiency in R, Python, or Tableau but also recognizing the nuanced competencies and attributes that set exceptional performers apart in the fields of data science and machine learning.

She delved into strengths such as reasoning, soft skills like communication and creativity as well, as understanding the intrinsic motivations that drive top talent in these specialized areas. This detailed mapping provided a plan of the kind of talent that Eager Analytics required.

Utilizing Specialized Channels
With an understanding of the skills, Maya guided her team towards more focused sourcing strategies. They explored job boards, connected with associations, and tapped into renowned academic networks known for producing exceptional data science and machine learning professionals.

Maya's team also made their presence known in places where their ideal candidates were likely to be found – from niche communities and forums to industry conferences and seminars. They engaged with rising stars and established experts alike, expanding their search beyond conventional boundaries.

Crafting Personalized Approaches

Recognizing the importance of attracting these sought-after professionals, Maya and her team created compelling pitches. They highlighted the work being done at Eager Analytics, the opportunities for career growth within the company, and the innovative culture that awaited new hires.

They emphasized the challenges and groundbreaking projects that candidates would have the opportunity to work on. This showcased how their contributions would drive advancements with impact. The messaging was carefully crafted to resonate with the motivations and aspirations of talents in this field.

The Results; An Influx of Qualified Applications

The outcomes achieved through Maya's approach were remarkable. By understanding the skills of identifying the appropriate channels and delivering personalized messages, Eager Analytics experienced a significant increase in applications from highly qualified data experts. Maya's efforts not only filled the talent gap but also established a strong and sustainable talent pool.

Lessons. Moving Forward...

Maya's experience in sourcing roles at Eager Analytics offers valuable insights. It emphasizes the importance of thoroughly mapping capabilities to determine the skills and qualities required. It highlights the effectiveness of leveraging platforms where niche talent gathers and engages. Lastly, it demonstrates the power of crafting personalized messages that resonate with the motivations of specialized professionals.

To summarize, successfully sourcing talent for niche positions requires a multifaceted approach. Maya's story illustrates that by combining capability mapping, utilization of specialized channels, and targeted communication, even highly elusive talents can be engaged and recruited.

CHAPTER 5
OPTIMIZING CANDIDATE EXPERIENCE

KNOWING THE CANDIDATE JOURNEY

Aaron's first day as the Vice President of Talent Acquisition at Glide Systems, a startup in the mobility industry, was quite eye-opening. He quickly realized that the company was facing challenges in its recruitment process. The sudden departure of the key recruiter had left the team feeling disoriented, and important engineering positions remained unfilled for extended periods. As Aaron dug deeper into the situation, he discovered an issue that was hindering the company's ability to attract talent; a seriously flawed candidate experience.

Uncovering the Root Problems
The candidate's experience at Glide Systems was alarmingly poor. Aaron discovered that job postings were filled with language that failed to communicate the roles and responsibilities. Communication with candidates was infrequent and slow, leading to feelings of neglect and frustration. The interview process was disorganized and lacked consistency, leaving candidates confused about their standing. To make matters worse, rejection messages were impersonal and uninformative, often leaving candidates with more questions than answers.

This inadequate management of the candidate's journey had consequences. Reviews on *Glassdoor* depicted a frustrating recruitment experience. The company witnessed a decline in offer acceptance rates, and employee referrals had dwindled due to negative experiences.

Embarking on a Journey of Transformation

Realizing the seriousness of these challenges, Aaron took it upon himself to completely revamp the Glide Systems candidate experience. He started by examining the journey from the candidate's perspective, using principles of customer experience design. This exercise uncovered pain points like application processes, unpredictable scheduling, and insufficient interview preparation. All of these contribute to an unwelcoming environment for potential talent.

Enhancing Key Interactions

Aaron's next step involved refining the interactions throughout the candidate journey. With his team, they reimagined job postings to highlight the work at Glide and warmly welcomed individuals from diverse backgrounds. They implemented approaches for scheduling and email communication to ensure promptness and consistency. Additionally hiring managers received training in interview techniques to bring consistency and professionalism to the interview process.

Even rejection messages were redesigned to provide feedback and maintain relationships. The team also introduced surveys to continuously gather feedback on the candidate experience, ensuring that Glide's values were reflected in every interaction regardless of whether or not someone was hired.

Observing Immediate Progress

The efforts began yielding results quickly. Glide Systems witnessed an increase in application rates and a significant 30% reduction, in the time taken to fill positions. Importantly, the acceptance rates increased significantly as candidates felt more appreciated and engaged throughout the process.

Fostering a Candidate-Centric Culture

However, Aaron knew that bringing lasting change required more than making process improvements; it called for a shift within the organization. He collaborated closely with top executives to enhance manager accountability for ensuring candidate experiences. Performance incentives were adjusted to include metrics related to candidate satisfaction. This strategic decision gradually instilled a sense of ownership and responsibility at all levels within the organization.

Achieving Success in Employer Branding

After a year of effort, the outcomes were outstanding. *Glassdoor* ratings for Glide Systems skyrocketed, reflecting the changes made in the recruitment process. Employee referrals bounced back, becoming a source of high-quality hires. Aaron's dedication to transforming the candidate experience not only rejuvenated Glide's employer brand, it also became an essential element of their overall talent strategy. The impact on business was undeniable as top-notch candidates now showed enthusiasm for joining and contributing to Glide Systems.

Aaron's journey at Glide Systems highlights the significance of optimizing the candidate experience in today's talent market. By understanding and enhancing each stage of the candidate journey, Glide transformed its recruitment process from being a weakness, into an advantage.

To optimize the experience for candidates, it is crucial to have a deep understanding their journey from initial outreach to onboarding, and beyond. It is important to put yourself in their shoes and consider every interaction they have along the way. By mapping out this process we can identify if there are any pain points. Then redesign it with simplicity and care.

Enhancing the Candidate Journey in Talent Acquisition
To excel in today's talent acquisition landscape, it is essential to have an understanding of the candidate journey. This encompasses every interaction a potential employee has with our organization, starting from when they come across a job posting until their first day on the job and even beyond that. By mapping out this journey we can identify any areas that may cause complexity or delays which could potentially lead to frustration for candidates. This enables us to create a positive experience overall.

Mapping Out the Entire Candidate Lifecycle
It is important to view the candidate journey as a whole by considering all stages of our recruitment process. This detailed mapping should cover:

- Initial Discovery and Application; The process through which candidates find job openings and submit their applications, including their impressions of our job postings
- Assessment; The phase where candidates go through evaluations such as, screening calls or assessments

- Interview Coordination and Communication; How interviews are scheduled, including reminders sent to candidates throughout the communication flow
- Interview Process Overview; This includes everything, from the preparation time given to candidates, the interview experience, and the follow-up afterward
- Notification of Hiring Decision; How and when candidates are informed about the outcome of their application
- Job Offer Procedure; The steps involved in extending, discussing and finalizing employment offers
- Communication Before Starting; Interactions that take place between accepting an offer and the first day on the job
- Welcoming New Hires on Their First Day; The orientation experience for hired individuals

Examining these stages helps identify obstacles or concerns that could adversely affect a candidate's experience.

Seeking Direct Input from Candidates
Obtaining feedback directly from candidates is vital for understanding their perspectives. This can be achieved through surveys sent via email, interview discussions, monitoring platforms like Glassdoor, and conducting exit interviews. We gain insights by asking questions about their motivations, impressions, emotional journey challenges faced, and suggestions for improvement. Actively listening to candidate feedback helps steer changes, in our recruitment process.

Experiencing the Journey Firsthand
A powerful way to understand the candidate experience is to have team members role-play as candidates, undergoing each

step of the process themselves. This approach involves applying for job positions, completing assessments, and participating in practice interviews with hiring managers. Experiencing the process firsthand often reveals insights that may be overlooked otherwise.

Measuring Key Recruitment Metrics
It is crucial to analyze recruitment metrics with a focus on the candidate's experience. Metrics such as completion rates, time-to-schedule interviews, interview attendance, response times to offers, and acceptance rates, can shed light on where candidates might be experiencing difficulties. These metrics help identify stages within the recruitment process that require refinement.

Observing Interactions in the Recruitment Process
Directly observing interactions between recruiters, hiring managers, and candidates provides an understanding of the experience. Observing how prepared hiring managers are for interviews, the quality of connections they establish with candidates, and how feedback is delivered, can reveal areas for improvement in communication and engagement.

Utilizing Candidate Personas
Understanding the journey from the candidate's perspective is essential. Candidates from diverse backgrounds, like software developers or teachers, will have varying expectations based on their professional experiences. Tailoring interactions to suit these different personas demonstrates an understanding of their unique perspectives.

Comparing with Competitor Practices

Comparing your recruitment processes with those practiced by competitors can offer valuable insights. Documenting and analyzing competitor practices can provide perspectives that help refine your recruitment strategies. By understanding how your process stacks up in terms of communication, interview experiences, and the overall speed of the process, you can identify areas where your organization can differentiate and improve.

Changing Candidate Perceptions

By mapping the candidate journey and backing it with relevant data and insights, organizations can uncover opportunities to positively transform candidate perceptions. Each interaction should be approached with simplicity and a human touch. This approach not only enhances the candidate experience but also strengthens the employer brand, making the organization a more attractive destination for top talents.

Understanding and optimizing the candidate journey is a process that involves examining every touchpoint during the recruitment cycle. By collecting feedback, simulating the candidate experience, analyzing metrics, and observing interactions, organizations can gain a comprehensive understanding of the candidate's journey. This understanding coupled with targeted enhancements can significantly improve the recruitment process. It leads to higher candidate satisfaction and, ultimately, a more effective talent acquisition strategy.

CREATING A POSITIVE JOURNEY

The candidate journey, from initial contact to the final hiring decision and beyond, plays a crucial role in shaping perceptions of an organization. However, it's not about understanding this journey; the real challenge lies in reimagining each interaction to create a memorable experience for potential hires. This means simplifying processes, improving communication, and consistently conveying your organization's values to candidates.

Making the Application Process Smoother

A complex or difficult application process can discourage interested candidates. To make this initial step smoother:

- Take advantage of technology to automatically fill in application fields whenever possible, reducing the effort required from candidates
- Minimize open-ended text fields in favor of structured inputs like dropdown fields, which can simplify data entry
- Enable auto-population of application fields from LinkedIn profiles or resumes to reduce repetitive information entry
- Concisely guide candidates through each step of the process ensuring they understand what is expected at every stage

Managing Scheduling Efficiently

Efficient scheduling is important for keeping candidates engaged. Implement systems that can seamlessly integrate with the calendars of recruiters eliminating the need for back-and-forth emails to find interview times. Additionally, these systems should be able to send automated reminders to reduce the occurrence of no-shows and facilitate rescheduling in case conflicts arise. The focus should be on prioritizing convenience and flexibility which demonstrates respect for the candidates' time and commitments.

Establishing Clear Communication Protocols

Establishing communication protocols is important in ensuring a smooth recruitment process. It is crucial to set service standards, such as responding to emails within 24 hours and promptly confirming interview appointments. Regularly monitoring and tracking response metrics can help ensure adherence to these standards. Furthermore, providing training to recruitment teams on maintaining a level of responsiveness is essential, as any delays or inconsistent communication can lead to candidate frustration.

Equipping Interviewers for Success

Equipping interviewers with the tools for success is vital as it significantly impacts the candidate experience. To ensure they are well prepared, it is important to provide them with background information on the candidates. Additionally, equipping them with insights into the needs of the position along with questions can facilitate meaningful dialogue during interviews. Regular training sessions for interviewers on best practices will further ensure they can effectively evaluate and engage candidates

Closing Feedback Loops

Creating feedback loops by establishing two-way communication channels is key in enhancing the recruitment process. It is beneficial to send structured debriefs post-interview to share impressions and gather feedback from candidates. Fostering a transparent and open dialogue can enhance the relationship even as candidates await final decisions.

Demonstrating Commitment to Inclusivity

Inclusivity should be a core element of the recruitment process. For example:

- Use inclusive language and imagery in job postings and other recruitment materials
- Provide training to interviewers and hiring managers to recognize and avoid unconscious bias
- Ensure that every aspect of the recruitment process reflects a commitment to diversity and equity

Showcasing Organizational Values

Values should be more than just slogans; they need to be demonstrated through actions. During candidate interactions, you can showcase these values by:

- Sharing stories and examples that highlight your organization's commitment to values such as innovation, caring, or integrity
- Ensuring that candidates have experiences of these values during their interactions with your team

Investing in Candidate Relationship Management

Implementing a **CRM** (Candidate Relationship Management) system can significantly enhance candidate engagement throughout the hiring process. This system enables:

- Personalized interactions at scale, ensuring the communications are tailored based on the previous engagements
- Automated distribution of relevant content to nurture relationships over time

- Continued engagement with candidates after a hiring decision has been made, building a talent pool for future opportunities

By following these practices you can create an environment that promotes inclusivity, showcases your values, and effectively manage candidate relationships throughout the recruitment journey.

By prioritizing responsiveness, transparency, and respect, at every stage of the candidate journey, organizations can greatly enhance how candidates perceive them. Achieving excellence in candidate experience goes beyond a recruitment objective; it becomes an advantage that sets an organization apart in the talent market.

BUILDING YOUR BRAND

When it comes to talent acquisition, the candidate experience goes beyond a series of steps. It serves as a tool for establishing and reinforcing your employer brand. Every interaction starting from the job posting to the interview, plays a role in shaping how people perceive your organization. A positive candidate experience can significantly bolster your brand, while any missteps can swiftly undermine it. It is crucial to ensure that marketing, communication, employees, and recruiting teams are aligned to effectively showcase your organization's culture and values.

Emphasizing Organizational Purpose

An employer brand hinges on communicating the purpose of your organization. The meaningful impact that your work has on customers and the community. In today's job market, candidates are increasingly seeking roles that offer more than a paycheck; they want their work to have significance. Incorporating your organization's purpose into career pages, job descriptions, and recruitment materials, is essential for attracting these candidates driven by purpose.

Reflecting an Authentic Culture
Authenticity plays an instrumental role in effective employer branding. One of the most persuasive ways to communicate your workplace culture is through testimonials from current employees. Allowing them to share their experiences and insights about the work environment, collaboration style, and growth opportunities within the organization carries more weight than generic corporate messaging ever could.

Highlighting the Importance of Diversity, Equity, and Inclusion
It is crucial to make your organization's Diversity, Equity, and Inclusion (*DEI*) initiatives visible. By showcasing your DEI programs, resource groups, demographic data, and commitment statements on platforms, you create an environment that is welcoming and supportive. This transparency plays a role in attracting a pool of candidates and demonstrates your dedication to fostering inclusivity in the workplace.

Harnessing the Power of Employee Advocacy
Encouraging employees to share positions within their networks can yield results. Provide them with sample posts and templates to simplify the sharing process and increase effectiveness. Personal referrals from employees carry credibility that traditional recruiting methods cannot match.

Effective Management of Online Reviews and Feedback
Taking a role in engaging with review sites like *Glassdoor* is essential for managing your employer brand. Regularly respond to reviews by expressing gratitude for feedback while constructively addressing any criticisms received. Acknowledging areas where improvements can be made, and demonstrating a commitment to implementing changes based on feedback, enhances transparency and builds trust.

Demonstrating Values through Real World Applications
Illustrate how your company's values are put into action, through projects and initiatives. Whether it's sustainability efforts, projects promoting product accessibility, or community volunteering activities - sharing these stories brings your values to life. Candidates are often drawn to organizations where they can see their values reflected in the work they do.

Promoting a Positive Image of Your Team
To showcase the vibrancy and diversity of your workforce, consider incorporating images, videos, and quotes, from team members on your career site and in job postings. It's crucial to create an environment where candidates can envision themselves fitting in and thriving. A key aspect of attracting talent is presenting a range of employees from different backgrounds in a positive light.

Engaging with Candidate Feedback
Seeking feedback from candidates through surveys, interviews, and reviews is important. Tracking metrics like Net Promoter Score can provide insights into how candidates perceive your organization. It's essential to refine your processes based on this

feedback to uphold and foster your reputation as an employer of choice.

Consistently Reflecting Your Employer Brand
Aligning every recruitment action with the desired perception of your employer brand is crucial. Throughout the recruitment process, candidates form their conclusions about your organization's culture and values based on their experiences. By reinforcing your employer brand at every touchpoint, you can craft a compelling narrative that resonates with employees.

From contact to onboarding, every step presents an opportunity to positively influence candidate perceptions and establish a strong appealing employer brand.

In this chapter we have explored the aspects of enhancing the candidate experience; understanding how candidates navigate their journey by creating an experience and establishing a strong employer brand. Each component plays a role in shaping candidates' perceptions and interactions with an organization. By integrating these elements, companies can greatly improve their talent acquisition strategies. To illustrate the implementation of these strategies we will delve into Aarons's experience as the VP of Talent Acquisition at Glide Systems.

Aaron's Challenge; Transforming the Recruitment Process
When Aaron joined Glide Systems, he faced challenges that were adversely affecting their ability to attract and retain talent. The recruitment process suffered from inefficiencies, lacked coherence, resulting in a poor candidate experience.

This was evident through *Glassdoor* reviews and declining offer acceptance rates. Recognizing the need for change, Aaron embarked on transforming Glide Systems' approach to candidate experience.

Mapping the Complete Candidate Journey
Aaron initiated a mapping exercise to identify every stage of the candidate journey. From the job discovery to their first day with the company, and beyond. This thorough process revealed pain points such as poor job descriptions, inconsistent communication practices, and disorganized interview procedures.

By going through the process as both a recruiter and a candidate, Aaron and his team gained experience of the difficulties and challenges that candidates were encountering.

Improving Processes and Communication
To tackle these issues, Aaron focused on making the application and scheduling processes more efficient. He introduced systems that made it easier for candidates to complete their applications and streamlined interview scheduling. Additionally, he established communication guidelines to ensure consistent interactions, with candidates. These changes not only made the process more candidate-friendly, but also demonstrated respect and appreciation for employees.

Creating a Positive Candidate Experience
Aaron then dedicated his efforts to creating a journey for candidates. This involved training interviewers, to engage effectively with candidates providing them with a positive

interview experience. He also implemented feedback sessions for candidates after interviews, fostering an environment of communication. The aim was to make every candidate feel valued, regardless of the outcome of their application.

Developing and Promoting Glide Systems Employer Brand
To enhance the Glide Systems' employer brand, Aaron undertook some major initiatives. He revamped job postings to accurately reflect the company's culture and values while attracting candidates who aligned with these principles. Aaron played a role in making sure that diversity, equity, and inclusion were not just buzzwords at the company. He made it a point to integrate these values into every step of the recruitment process making Glide's commitment visible to all. Additionally, he encouraged employees to share job openings and share their experiences at Glide, which helped attract candidates.

Another area where Aaron excelled was managing Glide Systems' online presence. He took the time to respond to reviews on platforms like *Glassdoor* addressing both criticisms and positive feedback in a similar manner. This showed that they were open to feedback and constantly striving for improvement.

Aaron's efforts had an impact on the organization. They experienced an increase in applications for job openings and reduced time to fill positions. They saw more candidates accepting offers. Employee referrals also increased significantly – an indication of satisfaction. As a result of Aaron's work, Glide Systems *Glassdoor* ratings improved significantly and their employer brand was revitalized.

The story of Aaron's journey at Glide Systems demonstrates how taking an approach to candidate experience can truly transform an organization. By understanding candidates' journeys throughout the recruitment process, and building an employer brand, companies can greatly enhance their appeal to potential employees.

This approach extends beyond filling positions; it establishes a strong reputation, as a desirable employer attracting highly skilled individuals and cultivating a supportive corporate environment.

CHAPTER 6
HARNESSING TALENT ANALYTICS

FOUNDATIONAL METRICS

At Vexus, a growing technology company, Priya, the Director of Talent Acquisition faced a hurdle. The CEO's directive to double the engineering team and meet product development deadlines created pressure for her and her team. Despite their efforts in finding and presenting candidates, the outcomes were far from satisfactory. Positions remained unfilled for months. When offers were made, they were often turned down in favor of more enticing proposals from competing companies. The lack of concrete, data-driven insights left Priya navigating through uncertainty, relying on experiences and varied opinions on the next steps.

In a move, Priya sought help from Vexus' data science team to analyze their talent acquisition processes. She granted them access to the team's tools and databases with the hope of gaining insights into their recruitment challenges. This collaboration marked a shift from strategies to a more analytical approach to talent acquisition.

The analysis conducted by the data science team revealed issues. Their heavy reliance on academic sourcing channels caused them to overlook engineers who were actively contributing to other companies. Additionally, their job listings lacked the specificity required to attract the talent that they needed. Most strikingly, the analysis revealed that their compensation packages were not competitive enough, causing them to lose potential hires to rivals.

With these insights in hand, Priya was finally able to address the weaknesses in Vexus's recruitment strategy. She diversified the sourcing strategy to include alumni from competitor companies, recognizing the value of experienced talent. The job descriptions were also revamped to communicate the technical challenges and opportunities at Vexus. Perhaps most importantly, she successfully advocated for enhanced compensation packages, understanding that competitive salaries were crucial for attracting candidates.

The impact of these data-driven changes was immediate and significant. The cost per hire decreased by 25% as the new sourcing strategies resulted in a candidate selection process leading up to job offers. The revised compensation packages led to an increase in offer acceptance rates. This transformation demonstrated how analytics can refine recruitment strategies and processes.

However, Priya realized that this marked the beginning of a journey. She expanded the scope of data tracking by including metrics on pipeline health, candidate progression rates, and interview effectiveness. Additionally, surveys were introduced to gather feedback from candidates enhancing their understanding of the candidate experience.

The success of these initiatives did not go unnoticed by Vexus leadership. Talent acquisition analytics quickly became a priority, throughout the company, as leaders from departments collaborated to brainstorm relevant data points and analytical questions. This marked a shift in Vexus's culture as analytics became a part of how the company approached talent acquisition.

The meticulous use of analytics during the recruitment process paid off immensely for Vexus. Within two years, the company not only achieved its ambitious hiring goals but also experienced substantial cost reductions in recruitment. Priya's talent acquisition team emerged as contributors during Vexus's hypergrowth phase proving the effectiveness of a data-driven approach to talent recruitment.

By transitioning from relying on intuition to adopting an analytical approach, the team was able to make well-informed and strategic decisions that greatly improved their recruitment outcomes. This chapter emphasizes the importance of metrics, advanced analysis techniques, and converting insights into strategies within talent acquisition.

In the fast-paced world of talent acquisition, it is crucial to leverage recruiting analytics by establishing metrics. These metrics serve as a benchmark to identify areas for improvement by shifting decision-making processes from assumptions to data-driven strategies. By tracking these Key Performance Indicators (KPIs), organizations can gain valuable insights into the effectiveness of their recruitment approaches.

Evaluating New Hire Success; Quality of Hire

One of the metrics in recruitment is determining the quality of hire. This involves assessing the performance of hired employees during their first 6 to 12 months. Key factors to consider include ramp-up time, early tenure productivity, and manager satisfaction ratings. By analyzing these patterns based on where candidates were sourced from, organizations can identify the most effective recruitment channels.

Monitoring Efficiency; Time to Fill

The duration between posting a job and accepting an offer is a metric referred to as "Time to Fill." Prolonged periods in this metric often indicate bottlenecks in the recruitment process, such as sourcing or lengthy interview stages. Comparing this metric against industry peers provides insights into process efficiency.

Understanding Recruitment Expenses; Cost Per Hire

Calculating the cost per hire is crucial for ensuring efficiency in recruitment practices.

This measure encompasses the expenses incurred for job postings, recruiter work hours, referral incentives, and other associated costs. These costs are then divided by the number of hires. Analyzing this expenditure across channels and teams can help identify areas where spending may be excessive.

Assessing Competitiveness; Offer Acceptance Rate

The offer acceptance rate refers to the percentage of job offers that candidates accept. This provides insights into an organization's competitiveness in the job market. Low acceptance rates might indicate issues with compensation or candidate experience. Monitoring this rate based on roles and teams can pinpoint specific areas that need improvement.

Evaluating Recruitment Sources; Channel Metrics

It is crucial to track metrics based on the source of the hiring channel. These include application volume, cost per applicant, screening pass-through rate, interview attendance, and the speed of offer delivery. This data helps identify which sourcing channels are most effective and efficient.

Strategic Hiring Planning; Workforce Planning Metrics

Workforce planning metrics play an instrumental role in looking at recruitment strategies. They involve analyzing projected hiring needs based on growth plans, and potential attrition rates and forecasting vacancy rates. By identifying gaps in roles, and setting goals for workforce composition, this proactive approach enables preparedness for hiring requirements.

Recruiter Productivity: Evaluating Team Performance

Assessing the productivity of recruiters involves measuring performance indicators such as the number of hires, and candidate interactions per recruiter per month. This analysis helps determine the effectiveness of both individuals and the entire team. By identifying team members who may require support or training, we can establish benchmarks for levels of activity. However, it's important to balance this with the risk of overburdening staff.

Candidate Satisfaction: Prioritizing Candidate Experience

To prioritize a candidate's experience, it is important to gather feedback from candidates about their journey throughout the recruitment process. By examining patterns that correlate satisfaction with factors like communication frequency, process speed, and interviewer professionalism, we can identify areas that need improvement.

Talent Pipeline Health: Ensuring Future Recruitment Success
Ensuring recruitment success relies on monitoring metrics related to the health of our talent pipeline. These metrics include assessing the volume of candidates at stages in the pipeline, predicting dates for prospects, and maintaining a balance between passive and active candidates. These indicators help us gauge whether our talent pool is robust enough to meet hiring demands.

By tracking these recruiting metrics, we lay down a strong foundation for more insightful analytics. Regularly monitoring these performance indicators not only reveals performance gaps but also presents opportunities, for improvement and optimization.

ADVANCED ANALYSIS

Moving from metrics to analytics, represents a crucial step in refining and enhancing the talent acquisition process. During this stage, recruiters employ techniques like data mining, predictive modeling, and text analysis to uncover insights to identify hidden patterns, and take advantage of emerging opportunities. This approach enables an understanding of the factors that drive recruiting effectiveness and guides strategic decision-making.

Data Mining; Uncovering Hidden Trends
The initial phase of analytics involves delving into existing metrics to reveal underlying trends and correlations. For example:

- Analyzing time-to-fill data can help identify bottlenecks in locations or roles, highlighting areas that require process refinement
- Exploring the connections between candidate satisfaction and tenure can offer insights into the long-term impacts of the recruitment process

Examining patterns within these metrics can provide insights that significantly enhance recruitment outcomes

Predictive Modeling; Forecasting Future Trends
Predictive models utilize historical data to predict future outcomes such as hiring needs, applicant quality, and the probability of offer acceptance. This proactive approach facilitates:

- Effective scenario planning, that enables recruiters to anticipate and prepare for challenges and opportunities
- Optimization of talent decisions by enhancing both the efficiency and effectiveness of the recruitment process

Utilizing Statistical Analysis
The Statistical methods offer an approach to delve deeper into recruitment data:

- Correlation analysis helps us understand the relationships between various recruitment metrics

- Regression analysis enables us to model the impact of different factors on recruitment outcomes
- Employing data normalization techniques ensures that any anomalies don't skew the results
- Significance testing provides a quantifiable level of confidence in the findings

Understanding Sentiments and Text Analysis
Text analysis techniques play a role in interpreting ended feedback. For example:

- By coding responses based on themes and sentiments, we can uncover the underlying emotions and concerns of candidates
- Analyzing the frequency and context of terms provides insights into candidate experiences and perceptions

Internal Benchmarking; Learning from Within
Comparing recruitment performance across business units, regions and teams within our organization allows us to:

- Identify best practices worth adopting and address shared challenges
- Highlight differences in hiring cycles between departments like engineering and sales or under varying market conditions

External Benchmarking; Putting Performance in Context
Looking beyond our organization at industry reports, and benchmark metrics from peer firms:

- Helps us establish realistic targets for our recruitment processes
- Provides context to industry data, enhancing our understanding of where we stand in the broader talent market

Market Analysis; Staying in sync with Industry Trends
By analyzing data from sources such as job listings and *LinkedIn* profiles, we can:

- Ensure that our recruitment strategy remains in line with the current availability of talent, compensation trends, and competitor strategies
- Keep our organization competitive and responsive to changes in the market

Collecting Qualitative Insights through Surveys and Interviews
Regularly conducting surveys and interviews with individuals involved in talent acquisition – candidates, employees, and hiring managers – allows us to:

- Gather qualitative feedback on what's working well and areas that need improvement in our recruitment process
- Adds depth to the data-driven insights, providing a more holistic view of the recruitment landscape

Encouraging Open Dialogue through Focus Groups
Organizing focus group discussions on aspects of talent acquisition enables us to:

- Foster dialogue and capture anecdotal insights that might be missed when relying solely on quantitative data
- Incorporate perspectives into our analysis with input from recruiters, technologists, and executives - each bring valuable insights

Putting Insights into Action
The true value of analytics lies in its application. Identifying opportunities for refining strategies, processes, and decision-making is just the first step. It's crucial to translate these insights into tangible actions that create meaningful impact. Whether it's making adjustments to how we find candidates, refining our interview methods, or rethinking how we engage with hires, every bit of insight is an opportunity to improve.

Advanced talent analytics is a powerful tool for transforming our recruitment strategies. By going beyond metrics and delving into data analysis, we can gain a deeper understanding of our recruitment processes. This enables us to make effective decisions.

FROM INSIGHTS TO IMPACT
In the field of talent analytics, the ultimate objective is not simply to gather insights but to effectively use these insights to improve and refine recruitment strategies, processes, and mindsets. The real value of analytics lies in its application. It is crucial to establish a well-structured approach, to applying insights to ensure that these insights result in tangible improvements.

Developing Action Plans Based on Analytical Insights
The process begins by creating action plans for each insight uncovered through analytics. These plans should comprehensively outline the implications of the insights, necessary changes, responsible individuals, required resources, potential risks, and how success will be measured. This level

of planning ensures a path from insight to implementation, solidifying the role of analytics in decision-making.

Methodical Testing and Scaling Changes

Before implementing changes on a scale, it is essential to validate them through pilot programs and A/B testing. Conducting small-scale tests allows us to confirm the effectiveness of proposed changes, and also provides an opportunity for adjustments, before the large-scale implementation. This structured approach helps mitigate risks and ensures that recruitment innovations are evidence-based and impactful.

Automating Analytics, for Real-Time Insights

To maximize the impact of analytics, it is important to integrate real-time data dashboards, set alerts for specific metric thresholds, and establish automated reporting workflows. This ensures that insights are gained and acted upon quickly, making data more accessible and actionable for recruitment teams.

Empowering Teams with Analytics Training

It is crucial to provide training to recruiters and hiring managers on how to use analytics. This includes teaching them how to interpret data, identify patterns, and apply insights in talent decisions. Through training, we can accelerate the adoption of analytics-driven practices throughout the recruitment process.

Aligning Recruitment Processes, with Analytics

We need to review and refine our talent acquisition processes – from sourcing to selection – to effectively integrate analytics. This might involve adjusting workflows to incorporate data collection and utilization of insights. The goal is to embed analytics deeply into the fabric of recruitment activities.

Cultivating an Analytics-Driven Culture

Creating a culture that values curiosity, inquiry, and data-driven experimentation is essential. Regularly communicating progress and successes achieved through analytics initiatives will inspire adoption. It's also important to celebrate instances where analytics have driven outcomes, as it encourages learning and adaptation based on data insights.

Structuring for Flexibility in Responding to Insights

Make sure that the structure and leadership approach in talent acquisition is agile enough to respond to findings from data analysis. Being flexible is crucial, as insights may lose their value if implementation is hindered by procedures.

Learning from Data-Focused Organizations

Gaining insights from organizations renowned for their data-focused approaches, such as technology companies and quantitative hedge funds can offer valuable lessons. Adapt their strategies like testing protocols, collaborations with data science teams, and models for analytics-driven leadership to enhance your practices.

Staying Updated on Emerging Techniques

Continuously embrace emerging techniques in talent analytics derived from research and industry advancements. Staying ahead of the curve in analytics can give you an edge in the evolving talent market.

Prioritizing Resources on Proven Strategies

Allocate resources to analytics initiatives that have demonstrated positive results. For example, if text analytics has proven effective in expanding the pool of candidates, it would be wise to invest in automated text processing tools. Let the data guide you on how and where resources are allocated for impact.

Unleashing the Potential of Talent Analytics involves embarking on a journey that encompasses gathering insights and implementing improvements driven by data.

To achieve better recruiting outcomes, organizations should adopt a mindset of learning and experimentation using data insights to drive improvements. This approach not only enhances recruitment processes but also paves the way for future innovations in talent acquisition.

In this chapter, we have explored the process of leveraging talent analytics starting from establishing measures and delving into analysis, and finally translating insights into meaningful changes within an organization. The story of Priya at Vexus, a growing technology company, serves as an example of how integrating these elements can transform the talent acquisition process.

Priya's Challenge; Overcoming Recruitment Obstacles
When Priya assumed the role of Director of Talent Acquisition at Vexus, she faced pressure to quickly expand the engineering team. Despite her teams' efforts, they encountered challenges. Hiring metrics were underperforming, job positions remained unfilled for months, and many candidates turned down offers. Without a data-driven approach, Priya found herself relying on experiences and guesswork.

Establishing Fundamental Metrics
Recognizing the need for an approach, Priya began by identifying foundational metrics. This involved tracking and analyzing indicators such as time required to fill positions, cost per hire, and acceptance rates for job offers. By establishing these metrics upfront, Priya laid the groundwork for a quantifiable understanding of Vexus's recruitment process.

Exploring Advanced Analytics
With foundational metrics in place, Priya and the data science team at Vexus embarked on a journey of advanced analytics. They utilized techniques such as analyzing data to uncover patterns in their hiring process, using models to anticipate their hiring needs, and the quality of applicants, and employing sentiment analysis to better understand candidate feedback. These efforts allowed Priya to gain an understanding of the shortcomings in their recruitment strategy.

Moving from Insights to Making a Real Impact
The insights derived from these analysis were truly enlightening. Priya identified inefficiencies in their sourcing methods, unappealing job descriptions, and non-competitive compensation packages. Armed with this knowledge, she took action. She expanded their sourcing strategies by targeting engineers from companies, revamped job descriptions to emphasize unique technical challenges, and advocated for improved compensation packages.

Revolutionizing Recruitment Performance
Implementing these data-driven strategies resulted in improvements within Vexus's recruitment process. The time

taken to fill positions decreased significantly, while the quality of hires improved noticeably as evidenced by higher offer acceptance rates, and enhanced performance among hires. Priya's approach revolutionized recruitment at Vexus by transforming it into an effective operation.

Establishing a Culture of Continuous Analytics
Priya's achievements at Vexus did not end with these changes. She consistently monitored a range of metrics including analysis of pipeline health and candidate satisfaction. Additionally, she fostered a culture of improvement and learning within the company. Her approach was not static; it was dynamic, adapting to new insights and market changes.

The executive team at Vexus took notice of the success achieved through Priya's analytics-driven approach. Recognizing its value, they decided to expand the focus on talent analytics throughout the organization. This shift marked a moment where analytics became deeply ingrained in the company's culture, transforming Vexus into not only a tech company but also an employer with a strong emphasis on data.

Priya's journey at Vexus exemplifies the impact that talent analytics can have. By starting with metrics and progressing to analysis, she was able to make significant improvements in the recruitment process by implementing changes based on these insights. This journey showcases how analytics can solve recruitment challenges, while also driving long-term strategic enhancements in talent acquisition.

CHAPTER 7
MARKETING YOUR OPENINGS

PROMOTING YOUR OPPORTUNITIES

In the world of organic retail, FarmFresh Produce had a strong desire to expand its chain of supermarkets rapidly. Aisha, who was in charge of hiring, played an instrumental role in this goal. She had the task of doubling the number of locations and staff within two years, to keep up with the increasing demand from customers. However, the existing recruitment strategy was not delivering results. The job postings were not attracting candidates, interviews were taking longer than desired, and job offers were often declined as other companies offered slightly higher pay.

Aisha quickly realized that a traditional approach of posting job openings and hoping for outcomes was insufficient for FarmFresh's growth plans. To address this challenge, she formed a project team consisting of professionals from marketing, public relations, and operations departments. Together they aimed to adopt a more strategic and data-driven approach to recruitment.

The team's initial focus was on analyzing exit surveys to understand why employees were leaving the company. They discovered some misconceptions that were costly for FarmFresh. Cashiers believed their working hours were inconsistent even though they followed set schedules; stockers felt there weren't opportunities for career advancement despite frontline development programs being available. It became clear that FarmFresh needed to improve its messaging by conveying the benefits and stability it offered as an employer.

Next, the team scrutinized application conversion rates by source, discovering that employee referrals had the highest success rate. They discovered that targeted advertising on niche job boards such as *RetailWire* is more effective than the general ones like *Monster*. This information was essential in deciding where to allocate the recruitment budget for impact.

Using this data, Aisha's team developed specialized outreach campaigns to attract candidates who were currently employed by competitors. They used channels to engage with candidates ensuring that FarmFresh stayed top of mind by providing them with relevant and interesting content. This approach proved significantly more effective than traditional job posting methods.

To further improve their recruitment efforts, they introduced a referral reward program which included incentives like gift cards, and bonus payouts for milestone anniversaries of referred hires. This initiative increased high-quality referrals massively expanding the pool of applicants.

The team was committed to a process of constantly testing and refining their strategies based on recruitment metrics. By customizing roles to specific locations, they saw an increase in the number of local applicants. Additionally, focusing messaging on benefits highlighted the company's commitment to employee stability. Leveraging employees as advocates in the media added authenticity and trustworthiness to their recruitment efforts.

Within a year it became evident that these focused efforts produced results for FarmFresh. The company has not only exceeded its ambitious hiring targets but the operations teams were fully trained in preparation for the opening of stores. Aisha successfully built an in-house recruitment system by giving importance to marketing, analytics, and operations. This comprehensive approach showed that successful sourcing required a combination of innovation, data-driven decision-making, and collaborative teamwork.

Aisha's experience at FarmFresh illustrates how integrating marketing tactics and data analytics into the hiring process can bring about results. By going beyond recruitment methods and implementing targeted strategies, the team significantly enhanced the quality and speed of their hiring efforts.

In today's job market, simply posting job openings and hoping for the best, is no longer effective. Effective job promotion now requires a proactive, data-driven approach that utilizes multiple channels to reach and engage ideal candidates. This involves utilizing channels to engage with candidates and showcasing your organization's unique culture and mission.

Using Social Media for Targeted Engagement

Social media is a tool for engaging both active and passive job seekers. Create targeted campaigns on platforms where your desired talent pool is most active. This includes:

- Following and interacting with candidates within your industry or field
- Encouraging employees to share job openings within their networks, expanding the reach organically
- Sharing content that highlights your company culture and values, making it an appealing place to work

Customizing Outreach Efforts

Personalization plays an important role in connecting with candidates. Develop outreach templates that can be customized for individual prospects, referring to their past companies, educational backgrounds, or specific experiences. Utilize automation tools to maintain communication over time while keeping it personalized.

Highlighting Your Team and Culture

Sharing stories, videos, and testimonials from employees can be highly effective in showcasing what makes your organization special. These should convey their passion for their work and the growth opportunities available at your organization. Encourage employees to be authentic brand ambassadors, sharing their experiences and the rewards of being part of the team.

Networking at Industry Events

One effective way to source talent is by attending industry events like conferences, meetups, university fairs, and community gatherings. When employees accompany you to these events, it not only helps in building networks but also provides a more personal platform to showcase your company culture and values.

Leveraging Employee Referral Networks
Don't underestimate the power of employee referrals when it comes to finding top-quality candidates. Encourage your staff members to refer candidates by implementing incentives such as bonuses or reward points for hires. Referrals typically result in candidates who are a better fit and have higher offer acceptance rates.

Targeted Advertising on Specialized Channels
Conduct research to identify niche sites, online groups, and industry publications frequented by your ideal candidates. Advertising on these channels tends to be more effective than using broad-based platforms like *LinkedIn* or *Indeed*. This targeted approach ensures that your job postings reach the audience.

Emphasizing the Role's Purpose
Your messaging should focus on the meaningful impact of the roles you are looking to fill. Highlighting how these positions contribute positively can attract individuals who align with your organization's values and mission. When it comes to making a difference in people's lives, promoting sustainability, or empowering clients messages that have a purpose, resonate deeply with top talent compared to generic corporate descriptions.

Establishing Meaningful Conversations
Engage potential candidates by positioning your outreach as the beginning of an ongoing conversation. This approach involves responding promptly to inquiries and providing valuable content, irrespective of whether candidates are ready to apply. This two-way communication demonstrates genuine interest in engaging with potential candidates.

Maintaining Detailed CRM Records
Make use of a Candidate Relationship Management (CRM) system to keep track of all interactions with prospects. This includes recording contact histories, shared content, and levels of engagement. A well-maintained CRM system is essential for nurturing relationships with candidates in a personalized and scalable manner.

Promoting job openings in today's market requires creativity, strategic planning, and a deep understanding of where your target audience spends their time. By empowering employees to become advocates for your organization, exploring targeted channels for advertising, and inspiring potential talent with purpose-driven messages, organizations can significantly enhance their recruitment efforts.

CRAFTING COMPELLING CONTENT

In the competitive landscape of talent acquisition, content is not just a medium of communication but a critical tool for attracting and engaging prospective candidates. It is essential to craft content that effectively showcases your organization's culture, empathizes with candidates, and inspires them. This process involves creating messages and materials that deeply resonate with your audience, aligning them with their personas and interests.

Highlighting Your People and Culture
It is vital to portray your organization's culture. Create genuine video and written profiles of current employees to give life to what it's like working at your organization. Encourage your staff to share their motivations and experiences – the things that keep them engaged and committed. There's immense power in peers sharing their lived experiences, offering a relatable and credible view of the work environment.

Bringing Organizational Values into Action
Illustrate how your company's values come alive through real-world initiatives. Share stories about product design influenced by accessibility, advocates, involvement in volunteering campaigns, or commitments to sustainability projects. These explicit examples help candidates visualize how these values translate into actions.

Clarifying Career Growth Opportunities
Career development prospects are an attraction for talent. Use short profiles to showcase the growth journeys of team members highlighting the development opportunities they have seized for advancement. Make sure to showcase a range of roles and career paths within the organization highlighting the avenues available for professional growth.

Transparently Spotlighting DEI Efforts
It is crucial to be transparent about your **Diversity, Equity,** and **Inclusion** (*DEI*) efforts. Share diversity statistics, pay equity

analyses, results from belonging surveys, and details about inclusion programs. Showcase staff members from diverse backgrounds, quantifying your commitment to creating an equitable and inclusive workplace.

Addressing Tough Topics Head-On
Address challenging topics directly and honestly. Communicate openly about how your organization handles obstacles such as layoffs, leadership changes, or setbacks in growth. By sharing insights into how you navigate adversity, you can establish credibility and authenticity as an employer.

Utilizing Diverse Content Mediums
Utilize a range of content formats like videos, images, infographics, and podcasts alongside text. Different mediums cater to preferences and learning styles while high-quality production can significantly boost engagement and appeal. It can also greatly enhance your credibility and authenticity as an employer.

Optimizing Job Post Language
Optimize job post language to attract candidates effectively. Use words that emphasize teamwork, problem-solving skills, and opportunities for skill development. Maintain a tone that welcomes individuals from all backgrounds.

Creating Posts for Easy Reading
When formatting job openings, it's important to make them easily readable. Use concise paragraphs, bullet points, bold headers, and highlight details. Also, ensure that the layout is mobile-friendly so that important information stands out and is readily accessible.

Customizing Content for Different Candidate Personas
Adjust the tone, topics, and calls to action in your content to suit different candidate personas. Technical talent may seek different information compared to creative roles, while marketing professionals may expect a different language style than those in sales. Personalizing your content can greatly enhance its relevance and impact.

Encouraging Employees to Contribute Content
Motivate your employees to contribute their ideas and insights in content creation. Provide them with templates and guidelines that streamline the process. Sharing stories and posts from team members not only builds credibility but also offers a real inside perspective, on what it's like working at your organization.

Effective employer branding relies on content as its foundation. Moving away from generic corporate communication, organizations should focus on crafting messages that are authentic, data-driven, empathetic, and genuine. This approach helps paint an appealing picture of the organization — one that resonates with candidates and inspires them to be part of your journey.

ADVERTISING AND OUTREACH

In today's job market, finding qualified candidates on a large scale requires a strategic approach that combines paid advertising, organic posting, and personalized outreach. This comprehensive strategy involves coordinating efforts, across platforms to ensure that your job openings effectively reach the right audience.

Paid Job Advertising Strategy
To expand the visibility of your job postings:

- Invest in targeted advertising campaigns on job boards, *LinkedIn*, and other social media platforms
- Customize your ads to focus on skills, experience levels, and relevant demographics for each position
- Utilize retargeting techniques to reconnect with previous applicants who have shown interest in your organization

Utilizing Specialized Job Boards
Identify and leverage industry job boards that align with your field and the specific positions you are trying to fill. For example:

- Technology-related roles can be advertised on platforms like *Dice*
- Academic positions may find a fit by posting on sites like *HigherEdJobs*
- Pharmaceutical sales roles could benefit from utilizing *MedReps*

Evaluate these websites based on their user-base suitability and volume on the roles you are advertising.

Optimizing *LinkedIn* Postings
LinkedIn plays a key role in job advertising. To make your job postings more effective, follow these guidelines:

- Create headlines and structure job descriptions
- Use relevant hashtags and keywords to increase discoverability

- Make sure the application process is simple and easy to understand

Reach out to Candidates Personally
Develop targeted outreach campaigns through channels like email, *LinkedIn InMail*, social media or even direct mail. Customizing your approach can significantly boost engagement with candidates.

Utilize Marketing Automation for Nurturing
Leverage marketing automation tools to deliver tailored content based on the interests and engagement levels of your prospects. Automation is key to scaling your outreach efforts effectively.

Engage Actively in Communities
Encourage your recruitment team to take part in forums, conferences, and niche online platforms that are frequented by your desired talent pool. Genuine engagement within these communities helps establish relationships and increases visibility.

Advertise on Industry-Specific Platforms
For certain industries, there are 'must-post' sites where top talent is known to search for opportunities. Failing to utilize these indispensable niche sites could mean missing out on high-quality applicants.

Collaborate with Hiring Managers
Involve department leads when creating job postings to ensure that the language and details resonate with candidates. Adding cross-functional input can greatly improve the appeal and relevance of your job advertisements.

Prioritizing Mobile Optimization
To prioritize optimization, it is essential to make sure that your career site, job listings, and application processes are mobile-friendly. This involves:

- Simplifying the application process, for users on devices
- Ensuring that job postings are easy to read and engaging on smaller screens

Retargeting Past Applicants
Maintaining ongoing communication with former applicants through relevant content can keep your organization top of their minds. When new roles arise that match their background, strategically retarget these candidates to re-engage them in your recruitment process.

Effectively promoting job openings in today's job market requires a combination of advertising, targeted outreach, and active community engagement. By integrating paid advertising with personalized communication, organizations can successfully attract the right talent.

In this chapter, we've explored the strategies, for marketing job openings. We've emphasized the need to promote opportunities, create captivating content, and implement advertising and outreach. To illustrate these strategies in action we'll look at Aisha's experience as the hiring manager at FarmFresh Produce during a period of growth.

Aishas Challenge; Scaling Up Recruitment at FarmFresh
Aisha faced the task of doubling FarmFresh Produces workforce and expanding their locations within a two-year timeframe. The

initial recruitment methods which relied on job postings and traditional approaches, proved ineffective in finding qualified candidates. They encountered challenges such as attracting candidates with grocery experience, difficulty scheduling interviews promptly, and a high rate of rejected offers.

Promoting Opportunities; A Data-Driven Approach
Recognizing that conventional methods were inadequate, Aisha and her team adopted a data-driven approach. They began by analyzing exit surveys to gain insights into misconceptions about job roles and career growth opportunities at FarmFresh. This valuable information allowed them to reshape their recruitment messaging to convey the benefits and opportunities offered.

Crafting Captivating Content; Showcasing FarmFresh's Culture
Next the team focused on developing content that genuinely reflected FarmFresh's culture and values. This involved creating videos, and written profiles of employees highlighting their enthusiasm for their work and the growth opportunities available within the company. They also emphasized FarmFresh's dedication to promoting diversity, equity, and inclusion (*DEI*), sharing statistics and program details transparently, which helped in positioning FarmFresh as an inclusive and progressive employer.

Effective Outreach Approaches
To expand their reach, Aishas' team utilized targeted job advertisements on job boards and social media platforms optimizing their job posts for engagement and discoverability. They developed outreach campaigns for candidates leveraging

marketing automation tools to efficiently nurture relationships. Additionally, they implemented referral reward programs that significantly increased the number of high-quality applicants through employee networks.

Continuous Testing and Refinement Implementation

The team's approach was more dynamic than static; it involved testing and refinement. Customizing roles based on locations, while emphasizing the benefits in their messaging, helped attract local applicants. Incorporating employee advocacy in media added a voice to their recruitment efforts.

Achieving Ambitious Hiring Objectives

These strategies yielded results. Within a year FarmFresh not only surpassed its hiring goals, but the operations teams were well-staffed and prepared for store launches establishing the company's recruitment strategy as a model of efficiency and effectiveness.

As we wrap up this chapter, FarmFresh's story serves as an example of how modern organizations can navigate the complexities of talent acquisition with success. In a job market where candidates have multiple options, standing out requires a sophisticated approach to job marketing – one that combines creative thinking, data-driven insights, and a deep comprehension of candidate preferences and behaviors.

CHAPTER 8
INTERVIEWING TO IMPRESS

PLANNING AN IMPACTFUL PROCESS

In the heart of Silicon Valley, surrounded by innovation hubs and start-up incubators, stood the headquarters of FutureTech. This company is well known for its state-of-the-art technology and its exceptional team. Our story begins on a Monday morning with Sarah Jennings, a recruiter with over ten years of expertise in the tech industry. She has earned a reputation as a talent scout possessing prophetic insights into human character. Today she faces the challenge of finding the right candidate for a vital role in FutureTech's latest project.

As Sarah sat in the conference room, sunlight streamed through the glass windows while she meticulously reviewed the candidates' resumes. She had posted a paid job on *LinkedIn*, and promoted that through her social networks. That promotion yielded a handful of impressive resumes.

Her keen eyes scanned each document not for skills and experience, but for subtle indications of personality and motivation that are crucial for success at FutureTech. The position is that of a Project Lead for an initiative driven by AI technology. The right candidate needed not only technical prowess but also exceptional leadership and innovative thinking.

Sarah's concentration was interrupted by her buzzing phone. It was Jack, the CEO of FutureTech checking in on her progress. "I have faith in your judgment, Sarah," he said reassuringly. "You've always had a talent for spotting potential that others tend to overlook," Sarah responded with a smile appreciating the compliment. "Thank you, Jack. I'm feeling optimistic about the interviews today" she confidently expressed.

The first candidate, Michael arrived promptly at 10 AM. He was impeccably dressed in a fitted suit and his resume showcased a range of experiences from renowned tech companies. However, as the interview progressed, Sarah sensed a lack of connection. Michael's responses, though technically sound, lacked the passion and creativity that FutureTech valued. It seemed like he was more focused on presenting his achievements than truly understanding the company's vision.

Up was Elena, a candidate with less experience. Her background was unconventional, with a mix of tech roles and humanitarian work. During the interview, Elena's eyes lit up with enthusiasm as she discussed her projects. She not only spoke about her contributions but also emphasized her efforts to foster teamwork and her genuine passion for leveraging technology to make a positive impact. Sarah recognized Elena's potential to bring perspectives to the team.

The afternoon brought forth a series of candidates, unique in their way; however, none quite resonated with Sarah in the desired way. As the day wore on, her focus began to wane, and the candidates started to blur together. But then, the last interviewee of the day, Alex, walked in.

On paper, Alex's resume wasn't remarkable. His experience was solid but not exceptional. He had attended a known educational institution. However, during the interview, Alex's strengths started to shine. He spoke candidly about his experiences, including his failures and the valuable lessons he learned from them. His problem-solving approach was innovative. He provided examples that showcased an understanding of teamwork and leadership in challenging situations.

What truly made Alex stand out was his curiosity about FutureTech's mission and his insightful inquiries about the challenges and objectives of the project. He engaged Sarah in a conversation that demonstrated his ability to think critically and collaborate effectively.

As the day ended, Sarah found herself reflecting on the day's interviews. While Michael brought experience to the table, and Elena displayed passion, it was Alex's rounded combination of skills, humility, and genuine interest in FutureTech's work that caught her attention. She realized that finding the candidate was not solely based on having a resume but rather, on embodying essential qualities for the role while aligning with the company values.

Sarah drafted her recommendation accordingly before sending it off to Jack. She knew that her choice might raise some eyebrows, given the unconventional pick, but she trusted her instincts. Through experience, she had come to understand that successful recruitment involved more than evaluating skills and experiences. It also required an understanding of the individual, behind the resume.

Effective planning plays a role, in organizing an interview process that thoroughly evaluates candidates and leaves them with an impression. It's important to establish evaluation steps that align with the position's requirements while maintaining a flow.

Map Competency Evaluations
Here are some key considerations for evaluating competencies during interviews:

- Proficiency and skills: This involves assessing qualifications such as software programming languages, statistical modeling abilities, writing expertise financial analysis knowledge, and more
- Problem-solving ability: Evaluate how candidates interpret information and assess alternatives and reach conclusions
- Communication style: Assess clarity, professionalism, listening skills and overall approach to communications
- Leadership and influence: If relevant to the role, look for evidence of motivating teams, mediating conflicts promoting ideas and driving change
- Teamwork and collaboration: Evaluate how candidates contribute when working collaboratively on projects or supporting colleagues as their commitment to collective goals, over individual accomplishments.

Assessing Alignment, with Values and Culture
Review the examples provided to determine whether the behaviors exhibited align with the stated values of the organization, such as excellence, respect, transparency, and fiscal prudence.

Establishing Interview Structure and Flow
Create a flow for interviews by designing a tailored set of assessment stages that meet your hiring requirements. This ensures an evaluation while maintaining a respectful process for advancing top candidates. For instance:

- Initial phone screening by the recruiter
- First interview conducted by the hiring manager
- Technical assessment phase
- Cross-functional panel interview
- Executive meeting to candidates with leaders
- Final decision discussion

Crafting Consistent Opening and Closing Statements
Provide interviewers with templates that guide them in initiating discussions by framing topics explaining the format and expectations as inviting candidate questions.

Closings should recap key discussion points and preview the next steps without introducing new topics that could catch candidates unexpectedly.

Developing Competency-Based Questions
Prepare a bank of questions directly linked to required capabilities that probe past experiences illustrating competencies in action.

Encourage follow-up questions to gather insights than simply following a fixed routine.

Questions should focus on eliciting examples of skill application rather than solely inquiring about credentials or technical trivia.

CRAFTING REVEALING QUESTIONS

Developing an interview process involves creating a collection of crafted questions that go beyond the information found on resumes. These questions should aim to uncover insights about a candidate's competencies, critical thinking skills, motivations, and cultural fit.

Create a Customizable Question Bank

Build a set of situational and technical questions that can be customized to fit your specific roles. Provide hiring managers with templates they can refer to and modify them based on the requirements for each position.

Explore Problem-Solving Abilities

Craft questions that present candidates with ambiguous business issues and ask them to describe how they would diagnose root causes, weigh alternatives, assess risks, and identify solutions. Evaluate not only the approach but also the clarity of their communication when responding. For instance;

"Imagine you are tasked with reducing manufacturing costs by 15%. How would you approach identifying opportunities and developing an action plan."

Highlight Resilience

Gain insights into how candidates have handled setbacks in their careers by asking questions such as;

"Tell me about a time when you aimed to achieve something at work but faced challenges in gaining support from stakeholders. How did you address their concerns?"

Assess their ability to overcome obstacles and mobilize support.

Unveiling Adaptability, in Learning

Ask candidates to share instances where they had to acquire knowledge or skills to make a significant impact on the business. For example;

"Tell us about a time when you had to educate yourself on a technology, system, or capabilities to achieve an ambitious goal."

Assess their speed, approach, and resourcefulness in improving their abilities.

Revealing True Motivations

Encourage candidates to envision their future within your company and discuss the milestones that would contribute most to their satisfaction. You can ask;

"If you see yourself thriving here five years from now, what factors do you believe will lead to your success and happiness?"

Compare their motivators with the drivers they express.

Addressing Potential Challenges
Guide the conversation towards uncovering any blind spots. For example, inquire why they are considering leaving their role, what flaws they acknowledge in their leadership abilities, or what feedback supporters and detractors from past projects might say about them.

There are no bad answers per se, but insightful risks, growth areas, or social self-awareness are revealed.

Developing Libraries of Follow-up Questions
Ensure that interviewers have prepared follow-up questions, for each scenario or experience shared by candidates. These can be used for exploration during the interview process.

This approach transforms interviews into dynamic conversations moving beyond the question-and-answer format. Strategically crafted, thoughtful questions allow interviewers to go beyond basic credentials and qualifications to gain insights into problem-solving, motivations, skill mastery, and culture fit. Develop expansive question banks to power impactful conversations.

MASTERING DELIVERY

Apart from asking crafted questions, the effectiveness of an interview heavily relies on the interviewer's delivery skills to facilitate two-way conversations. Technique matters greatly, from active listening to projecting genuine interest while being aware of personal biases.

Active Listening
Give your attention to what the candidate is saying without thinking ahead to the next pre-planned question. Pay attention to cues in their tone, body language, and speech patterns for underlying messages. Allow space for candidates to elaborate rather than dominate discussions or over-talking them.

Demonstrate Engagement
Use encouraging expressions, positive verbal feedback, and open body language. Avoid distractions that might signal disengagement. Candidates gain confidence and open up more when the interviewer visibly shows interest in their responses. This creates an exchange of ideas.

Allow Sufficient Time for Responses
Avoid cutting candidates off after asking a question; wait for 7 to 10 seconds before jumping in. Thoughtful responses require time for candidates to gather examples and articulate their points. Silence may feel uncomfortable at times. Being patient yields insights that rushed answers won't provide. Repeating back on what you hear shows listening.

Clarify Before Providing Feedback
Before critiquing a candidate's response, rephrase what you understood them to say first. Sometimes candidates may express themselves imprecisely. Make sure you accurately capture their intended message before assessing the merit of their responses.

Follow Up Rather Than Follow Script
Rather than following a predetermined script, it is more effective to actively listen to candidate responses and explore

interesting avenues for further discussion. Their initial examples may reveal competencies exploring in depth, rather than just moving on to the next planned question. Prioritize understanding and meaning over structure.

Mitigate Personal Biases
When someone begins speaking, it's important to recognize and manage any negative reactions that may arise due to personal biases. Take a moment before reacting and strive to understand the perspectives being expressed. Assess the merits of their thoughts separately from your biases. Even if you disagree, maintain a neutral body language before seeking clarification.

Set Expectations Upfront
At the beginning of the interview, communicate the topics you plan to cover, provide an estimated timeline, and indicate opportunities for candidates to ask questions at designated points. This helps alleviate anxiety for candidates and also encourages them to freely share their thoughts. Establishing clear expectations upfront is beneficial.

By focusing on connecting with candidates through equitable communication, we can uncover valuable insights that contribute to excellent hiring decisions. Aim for interactions that go beyond question-and-answer exchanges.

As we come to the end of this chapter, let's reflect on Sarah Jennings's journey, at FutureTech and how her thought-out recruitment approach led to successful outcomes. Her story beautifully connects the three sections of this chapter; Planning an Impactful Process Creating Revealing Questions and Mastering Delivery.

Sarah's careful planning laid the groundwork for the recruitment process. She identified the platforms for targeted advertising, utilized specialized job boards, and optimized FutureTech's presence on *LinkedIn*. This comprehensive approach during the planning phase played a role in attracting a pool of highly qualified candidates. Sarah's strategy was not about reaching as many people as possible; it focused on reaching out to the right individuals. The influx of top-notch candidates that Sarah witnessed was a result of her targeted planning.

The next phase of Sarah's strategy involved formulating questions that were both revealing and insightful. This is where her deep understanding of the role and company culture came into play. Sarah developed a set of questions that went beyond aspects and aimed to uncover candidates' problem-solving abilities, adaptability, and alignment with the company culture. These questions were customized for each candidate ensuring that every interview was an opportunity to explore the candidate's strengths, weaknesses, and potential.

Sarah's final step, in her recruitment strategy involved mastering the art of conducting interviews. Her approach was empathetic and engaging. She made sure that each candidate felt valued and understood creating an environment where they could showcase their abilities. Sarah's skill in making candidates feel comfortable and her ability to navigate conversations effectively to gather information turned each interview into a dialogue rather than just an evaluation process.

As the recruitment campaign reached its climax, Sarah's hard work paid off. The perfect candidate for the Project Lead position emerged as a testament to the success of Sarah's strategy. This candidate not only possessed proficiency but also perfectly aligned with FutureTech's culture exhibiting qualities such as leadership, creativity, and a collaborative spirit that Sarah had astutely identified through her process.

Looking back on her journey, Sarah acknowledged the effectiveness of an integrated approach to recruitment. The success of her campaign went beyond simply filling the vacancy; it affirmed that a planned and thoughtfully executed process could yield better outcomes.

CHAPTER 9
INNOVATIVE ASSESSMENTS

SIMULATIONS AND EXERCISES

As the sun rose in the early morning sky, its warm rays enveloped the New York skyline signaling the start of another day of possibilities. Eva Chen, the Head of Talent Acquisition, at Vertex Innovations sat in her office located in the heart of the city gazing out at the streets. Today marked a moment for her as she embarked on an endeavor to revolutionize Vertex's recruitment process.

Known for their trailblazing advancements in technology, Vertex was now entrusting Eva with the task of aligning their recruitment strategies with their spirit. She understood that traditional interview and assessment methods would no longer suffice when it came to finding individuals who possessed not only expertise but also adaptability, creativity, and forward-thinking.

Eva's mind buzzed with ideas as she pondered how to replicate the challenges of the tech world within their recruitment process. She envisioned creating scenarios that mirrored the intricacies and unpredictability of real-life projects at Vertex. Candidates would be invited to step into roles such as project managers or lead developers and navigate through crafted simulations designed to test their skills, problem-solving abilities, and aptitude for leadership under pressure. These exercises aimed to provide more than assessments; they offered glimpses into candidates' future performance and potential.

As Eva delved deeper into her planning she started thinking about the value of insight when evaluating a candidate's suitability. Why limit the assessment to the hiring team when you can tap into the wisdom of the crowd? Eva envisioned a platform where tech experts, industry professionals, and even future colleagues could contribute their perspectives on candidates' solutions to challenges. This collaborative approach would not only make the evaluation process more inclusive but also provide a comprehensive understanding of a candidate's abilities and openness to constructive feedback.

In addition, Eva pondered the potential of evaluation technologies. In a world without boundaries for talent, she imagined utilizing software and AI-powered analytics to assess candidates on a global scale. These tools wouldn't only evaluate skills; they would also analyze patterns, virtual collaboration in teams, and even how well candidates adapt to remote work. It wasn't about accessing a pool of talent; it was about embracing the future of work and evaluation.

As she pieced together her forward-thinking strategy, Eva felt a sense of excitement. These innovative assessment methods went beyond recruitment tools; they exemplified Vertex Innovations' dedication to staying ahead of industry trends. They aimed to assess the candidates' capabilities through forward-thinking methods.

Traditional interviews often fall short in predicting job performance. To gain insights, into candidates' skills and decision-making abilities, it is beneficial to incorporate assessments that involve hands-on simulations and exercises mirroring real work scenarios.

Develop Realistic Job Previews
One effective approach is to create job previews. This involves crafting roleplay scenarios where candidates are placed in situations they would encounter if they were hired. For example, for customer service roles they could be asked to troubleshoot a complaint from a customer. For managers, the scenario could revolve around resolving tensions between team members. By observing how candidates approach these situations and come up with solutions, their competency mastery can be gauged.

Assemble In-Baskets
Another method is using '*in baskets*'. Candidates are given a collection of emails, and memos, and asked to prioritize based on what they would handle in a week if hired. They are then asked to process these items while assessing their importance, delegation opportunities, and any information required, and finally determining the steps to take. This evaluation helps assess their ability to prioritize tasks logically, allocate time effectively, and ask follow-up questions when needed.

Build Presentation Challenges

Including presentation challenges can also provide insights. Candidates may be assigned a strategic business topic, and be given a 12 or 24 hours notice to prepare a short presentation on it. They can incorporate company data as needed that are in the public domain. This assessment allows observers to assess where candidates focus their attention during the presentation, the insights they highlight, as well as the clarity and conciseness of their delivery. It also provides an opportunity for Q&A sessions.

Develop Specialized Demo Opportunities

Lastly, specialized demo opportunities tailored for various functions can be developed. For training roles, candidates can be requested to conduct demo lessons; for marketing-focused positions, designing a social media campaign could be assigned; while developer positions may require coding a feature for an app. These tailored opportunities aim to provide evidence of competencies in action that are specific to each function rather than relying on general simulations.

By incorporating these assessment methods, employers can gain a comprehensive understanding of candidates' abilities and make informed decisions during the hiring process.

Encourage Discussions

In the panel interviews, introduce unexpected business strategy dilemmas or trending topics that candidates are unlikely to have prepared for in advance. This allows us to assess their ability to stay composed under pressure, their problem-solving instincts, and their communication skills when caught off guard.

Compare Leadership Traits with Individual Contributor Traits

When interviewing both manager and non-managerial candidates, design different simulation exercises to evaluate leadership behaviors such as delegation, influencing, and conflict resolution. Additionally, assess individual contributor qualities like thinking, task execution, and attention to detail. Tailor these simulations according to job roles.

Measure Interview Performance Quantitatively

Evaluate the performance in simulations based on clearly defined grading criteria such as prioritization effectiveness, identified insights, engagement levels, conciseness of responses, and other attributes aligned with success factors of the role. Compare these observations from the simulation with impressions from interview conversations.

Continuously Expand Your Collection

Consider developing simulations as an ongoing effort. Continually create scenarios that reflect emerging priorities and challenges faced in various roles. Rotate these scenarios among candidates while ensuring various simulation experiences over time. This prevents candidates from being prepared by practicing the same simulations.

Immersive and sophisticated assessments provide insights into performance that traditional interview questions cannot capture alone. Simulations demand a demonstration of capabilities for success in a specific role.

CROWDSOURCED ASSESSMENTS

To gather perspectives and avoid distorting decisions, it is beneficial to involve a wide range of assessors when evaluating candidates. This can be achieved through crowdsourcing evaluations from a panel of assessors. Additionally, modern platforms provide flexible ways to conduct assessments.

Seek Internal Stakeholder Feedback

To gather feedback from stakeholders, it is recommended to arrange meetings between candidates and potential future colleagues or direct reports. These conversations should focus on understanding the candidate's communication style, service mentality, leadership presence, and other relevant aspects. Feedback forms can be used to collect ratings and qualitative impressions enabling viewpoints to contribute to an assessment.

Conduct Peer Interview Panels

Another effective approach is conducting video interviews with employees who have been trained for this purpose. This helps streamline the screening process by standardizing conversations through peer panels. As a result, recruiters and hiring managers can devote time to in-depth engagements with several finalists. It is advisable to crowdsource this step at a scale.

Automate Skills Testing

When assessing candidates' skills, leveraging testing platforms such as *HackerRank* or *Codility* can be highly beneficial. These platforms administer assessments that measure technical proficiency, coding abilities, and other skills assessments at scale. By automating the skills testing process, objectivity can be enhanced.

Structure Consistent Assignments

To ensure comparisons among candidates for a role, it is recommended that all candidates complete the same simulation assignments using structured platforms. Examples of these assignments could include analyzing data sets to present findings or creating presentations that showcase communication abilities. Another option could involve submitting designs that demonstrate creativity, in problem-solving scenarios. Standardization allows for equitable comparison.

Enable Anonymous Peer Feedback

Enable the option for employees to provide feedback on work samples such as writing excerpts, proposed strategies, or presentations without being aware of the candidates' credentials. This approach ensures that the focus is on the quality of work rather than any biases. Wherever possible anonymize assessment evidence to reduce bias further.

Seek Crowdsourced Referrals

Actively reach out to networks and online communities to request referrals for priority roles. Specify the required capabilities for these positions. Follow up with all prospects suggested, even if they may not be a match. By leveraging crowdsourcing, we can identify candidates who might have otherwise been overlooked.

Implement Automated Chat Interviews

Incorporate AI-enabled chat interview platforms like *Mya* (acquired by The StepStone Group) and *Olivia* (acquired by Nubank) during the screening stages. These chatbots assess candidates through text or voice conversations. Analyze their responses for competencies. The use of automated interviews allows us to gather insights from a pool of applicants more efficiently.

Leverage Gig Community Platforms
Gathering evaluations from a variety of assessors through crowdsourcing allows for a range of perspectives while also minimizing the influence of hiring manager biases. The use of platforms further enhances the flexibility of assessments. Leveraging 360-degree feedback leads to informed decision-making.

ADVANCEMENTS IN REMOTE EVALUATION

Remote and virtual assessments provide employers with the opportunity to evaluate a pool of candidates while offering flexibility. Recent advancements have also made it possible to conduct proctoring, video analysis, and even initial AI screening all aimed at streamlining the assessment process.

Conduct Skills Testing Under Live Supervision
One approach is to have candidates complete skills tests such as coding, data analysis, writing ability assessments, or design challenges. These tests can be conducted under supervision by proctors who monitor candidates in time through webcams and screen sharing. This method helps prevent cheating risks and ensures the measurement of abilities.

Automate Proctor Authentication
To authenticate test takers before assessments, platforms like *ProctorU* and *Examity* employ scans, government ID

verification, and human reviews. This robust authentication process mitigates the possibility of candidates using proxies or substitutes during the assessments. Strict identity checks are implemented to maintain credibility.

Use Anti-Cheating Algorithms
Skills testing platforms employ anti-cheating algorithms to analyze factors such as typing patterns, web activity, eye movements, etc. to identify actions that may indicate answer sharing or internet searches. AI-powered assessments compare responses against baselines to detect anomalies and safeguard integrity.

Analyze Video Responses with AI
Furthermore, platforms like *SparkHire* and *HireVue* utilize artificial intelligence, facial analysis techniques with tone evaluation, and linguistic processing on video-recorded responses. These analysis assess engagement levels, knowledge states, non-verbal cues, and clarity of communication. This innovative use of AI expands upon what traditional interviews cannot uncover.

Design Custom Virtual Simulations
Create personalized simulations that candidates can complete remotely. These simulations will involve tasks such as analyzing business datasets, writing sample reports, developing strategy briefings, or designing prototypes. The simulations will closely resemble work challenges. You can use cloud collaboration spaces to host the simulation delivery and review process.

Structure Live Video Panel Interviews

Organize video panel interviews where candidates have the opportunity to meet with a series of interviewers in condensed 60 to 90-minute discussions. During these panel discussions, they can discuss a shared case study, or present their sample work. While the panelists collaborate behind the scenes to evaluate responses, video technology allows for concentrated group evaluations.

Facilitate Remote Assessment Centers

Over multi-day schedules, candidates participate in extended skills evaluations like leaderless group discussions, behavioral interviews, presentations, roleplays, and more, conducted fully online. You can utilize sophisticated video conferencing platforms to deliver these assessments replicating the traditional live experience.

Train Internal Staff as Video Interviewers

Train staff members across business units to become proficient video interviewers. This will be accomplished by providing them with 30-minute video interview guides and conducting training sessions to align expectations and norms. Distributing interviews across broader reviewer pools through video conversations can help scalability.

Technology enables more data-driven, flexible, and efficient external assessment while reducing risks like cheating and bias. Video expands conversational evaluations while AI supports analysis not possible manually. The next frontier lies in the delivery of assessments, through channels simultaneously.

As the sun sank below the horizon casting a glow over the bustling city, Eva Chen found herself sitting in her office at Vertex Innovations, deep in thought about the incredible journey she had embarked on. The task of revolutionizing the company's recruitment process had been both challenging and thrilling taking her and her team on an adventure of exploration and creativity.

Eva's mission was to introduce a perspective to talent acquisition that aligned perfectly with Vertex's cutting-edge values. Her approach was diverse, breaking away from the traditional recruitment methods and venturing into realms of assessment techniques.

The first step in Eva's strategy involved implementing a series of simulations and practical exercises. These were carefully designed not only to assess expertise but also to immerse candidates in situations that closely mirrored the complex realities they would encounter at Vertex. Working closely with project managers and technical leads, she crafted these simulations to accurately reflect the challenges and opportunities within the company.

Candidates were given the opportunity to lead simulated projects through their lifecycle - navigating budget constraints, managing team dynamics, overcoming technical obstacles, and adapting to shifting project goals.

These exercises offered insights into the candidates' critical thinking abilities, their adaptability to changing situations, and their ability to lead with confidence and empathy. The simulations also provided an opportunity for the candidates to showcase their thinking and problem-solving skills in time, which is something that traditional interviews cannot fully capture.

The second aspect of Eva's approach involved using crowdsourced assessments. This unique method utilized the expertise of a community beyond just the immediate hiring team. Candidates' work and solutions were shared on a platform where industry experts, peers, and potential future colleagues could review and offer feedback.

This crowdsourcing technique provided an evaluation of the candidate's technical skills, creativity, and ability to respond constructively to criticism. It also allowed Vertex to assess how well candidates aligned with industry standards and practices. This method proved insightful as it added layers of depth to the evaluation process by revealing aspects of the candidate's skills and personality that might have otherwise remained hidden.

The final component of Eva's strategy was integrating evaluation tools. Recognizing the nature of talent acquisition and the growing trend toward work, Eva leveraged cutting-edge technology to assess candidates from around the world.

She utilized AI-powered tools to analyze how candidates performed in tasks including coding exercises and virtual group collaborations. These tools provided data-driven insights into candidate's technical skills, their ability to communicate effectively, and how they approached problem-solving. This technology ensured evaluation focusing solely on the merits and abilities of the candidates.

As Eva assessed the results of this recruitment approach, she felt a sense of accomplishment. The quality of candidates that emerged from this process surpassed what traditional methods had achieved in the past. The simulations and practical exercises revealed individuals with problem-solving skills and leadership potential. By incorporating assessments a wide range of perspectives enriched the evaluation process unveiling talents among applicants.

Moreover, this innovative approach resonated positively with the candidates themselves.

Many individuals have expressed their enthusiasm and sense of renewal towards the process appreciating the chance to demonstrate their skills in an authentic environment. This positive experience for candidates has significantly bolstered Vertex's reputation in the job market by establishing the company as a forward-thinking employer.

As Eva concluded her work for the day, shutting down her laptop and dimming the lights in her office she could feel that this was the beginning. The realm of recruitment was transforming with Vertex Innovations leading from the frontlines. The journey she embarked upon has paved paths for talent acquisition – paths that hold potential to propel Vertex to unprecedented heights of achievement and ingenuity.

CHAPTER 10
BUILDING A WORLD-CLASS RECRUITING PROGRAM

STRATEGY AND PLANNING

In the heart of San Francisco where ambition and innovation converge, stood the yet distinguished headquarters of Orion Tech. Within its walls amidst the buzzing atmosphere of creativity sat Emily Johnson, leading the Talent Acquisition team. Today Emily faced a challenge that would redefine her career; designing and implementing a world-class recruitment program for Orion Tech. This task went beyond hiring needs; it aimed to shape the company's workforce.

Emily had been a part of Orion Tech's journey from its beginning as a startup to its current position as a prominent player in the tech industry. However, with the company on the cusp of growth, she recognized the imperative for a transformation in their recruitment strategy. The goal was not to attract top-tier talent but to establish a system that nurtured enduring relationships, with potential candidates in an intensely competitive market.

On this morning Emily's mind brimmed with ideas and countless possibilities.

Initially, Emily focused on devising an encompassing recruitment strategy driven by data. This meant evaluating every facet of Orion Tech's existing approach; identifying strengths and pinpointing areas primed for innovation. While this phase seemed daunting, Emily remained resolute in her determination.

Emily's strategy started by examining market trends and analyzing the changing job landscape to identify the skills for the future. She meticulously studied recruitment metrics to assess how effective their current hiring methods were and had in-depth conversations with department heads to align the recruitment plan with the company's business goals.

One important realization for Emily was the need to shift from a reactive to a proactive talent acquisition approach. Rather than waiting for vacancies to arise, Orion Tech needed to anticipate future hiring needs and build a talent pipeline in advance. This involved strengthening their employer brand and engaging with candidates through diverse channels, nurturing connections even before specific positions become available.

Emily also aimed to broaden their recruitment sources beyond platforms. They explored niche forums, professional networks, and academic partnerships. This approach would not only diversify their candidate pool but also position Orion Tech as an employer of choice in various professional circles.

Improving the candidate experience was another aspect of her strategy. Emily acknowledged that candidates today evaluate employers as much as they are being evaluated. She envisioned a recruitment process that was not only efficient and transparent but also engaging and reflective of Orion Tech's culture.

In her planning, Emily gave importance to metrics and data analytics. She wanted to make sure that every aspect of the recruitment process should be measured, allowing for evaluation and improvement.

Emily then turned her attention to the human element of the recruitment process - the recruiters and interviewers. She believed that a team of skilled, culturally aligned recruiters was critical for the success of the program.

She looked for individuals who not only had talent acquisition expertise but also had a passion for technology and were exceptional at building relationships. Continuous learning and development were elements of her plan ensuring that her team stayed updated with the industry trends and recruitment techniques.

Emily created a training program for interviewers across Orion Tech. This program was designed to hone their skills in evaluating candidates for both technical and cultural fit. It included sessions on reducing bias, mastering effective interviewing techniques, and creating a positive experience for candidates.

Furthermore, she standardized the interview process by establishing consistent criteria for evaluating candidates. This approach aimed to ensure fairness and consistency in assessing candidates regardless of which department they applied to.

The final part of Emily's strategy was incorporating technology to improve and streamline Orion Tech's recruitment process. She envisioned a cohesive talent technology ecosystem that was intuitive, efficient, and candidate-friendly.

Emily explored solutions, including advanced Applicant Tracking Systems (ATS) and AI-powered sourcing tools, and even considered the potential of virtual reality for immersive job previews. Her focus was on technologies that could automate routine tasks, allowing her team to engage more meaningfully with candidates.

She also acknowledged the importance of data analytics in making recruitment decisions. Emily intended to leverage data from the ATS and other sources to gain insights into the effectiveness of recruitment channels and understand candidate behaviors and preferences.

Another innovation in her plan was enhancing the capability for remote interviewing and onboarding. With a talent pool that spanned the globe, Emily was keen to ensure that Orion Tech's recruitment was as effective for remote candidates as it was for local ones. This involved investing in quality video interviewing tools and creating an engaging and comprehensive virtual onboarding experience.

As the day came to an end and city lights twinkled outside her window, Emily reflected on her plan. It went beyond being a recruitment blueprint; it served as a roadmap, for building a workforce that could drive Orion Tech's growth and innovation in its phase.

Knowing that the road ahead would be filled with challenges she decided to switch off her desk lamp and venture out.

A top-notch talent program begins with a recruitment strategy and careful planning to ensure that hiring efforts align with the business objectives. It is essential to establish a vision, investment philosophy, and governance framework that prioritizes the importance of people in driving success.

Clearly Define Your Mission
Craft a compelling mission statement that reflects the organization's aspirations for talent recruitment. This statement should encompass elements such as:

- A commitment to attracting, developing, and retaining individuals who contribute to executing the business strategy
- A promise to build motivated teams that drive growth
- A vision for fostering career paths within the organization
- Positioning recruitment as a capability that provides an advantage through exceptional talent acquisition

A concise mission statement will anchor your efforts in long-term aspirations rather than mere annual hiring targets.

Align Workforce Plans with Business Priorities
Forecast future hiring needs by connecting them to goals such as revenue generation, product innovation, service quality,

and productivity. Map out programs and initiatives based on the required roles, competencies, and team development for delivery. Integrate talent planning into overall annual planning to align focus.

Invest Wisely Based on Impact
Categorize strategic business units, functions, and project teams according to their financial impact, customer impact, and innovation potential. Allocate recruiting resources proportionally by prioritizing involvement in personalized sourcing strategies and premium branding efforts for roles that provide value at an enterprise level. Treat the highest potential hires as uniquely as your highest value customers. Design the overall budget to mirror the business impact.

Structure for Agility
Implement a forecasting system that allows for resource allocation leveraging variable recruiters, contractors, and on-demand support to quickly scale capacity based on changing priorities. This approach will allow us to adapt to the hiring demands of emerging initiatives as they gain momentum and become a priority. At the same time, it will help us avoid unnecessary costs during stable periods.

Effective Governance through Cross-functional Collaboration
Establish centralized recruitment governance forums for capability planning, investment allocation/optimization, policy setting, and program oversight. Cross-functional councils ensure consistency, provide hiring manager support, and enable divisional collaboration solving shared challenges like niche skills sourcing rather than fragmented efforts.

Balancing Standardization and Customization
Find the balance between processes and localized customization for optimal performance. Centralized teams can define process standards, technology platforms, policies, and scorecards that are applied across groups while allowing flexibility to meet needs. It is important to establish standards without burdening everyone with uniformity. Exceptions should be based on business logic rather than freely granted.

Continuous Analysis of Market Dynamics
Constantly monitor talent availability costs, competitor pay benchmarks, and employer brand perception as inputs for strategy adjustments. Just as product leaders obsess over changing customer preferences, we need to track shifts in candidate expectations fluctuations, in sourcing channel ROI (Return on Investment), and the evolution of our talent pool.

Developing and planning a recruitment strategy enables talent leaders to contribute to the success of the business. It also helps in motivating teams by uniting them around inspiring goals that go beyond headcount metrics.

GREAT RECRUITERS AND INTERVIEWERS

Creating a top-notch talent program requires recruitment professionals and interviewers who possess the expertise to attract, evaluate, and persuade candidates effectively. It is crucial to establish support systems, learning opportunities, and vocal advocates to maximize the impact of sourcing efforts.

Nurturing Sourcing Specialists

We should avoid assuming that all recruiters excel in every aspect of their role from managing high-volume job postings to executing outreach campaigns and building niche communities. Instead, we should focus on developing sourcing specialists who possess an understanding of targeted proactive talent mapping and outreach. This specialization allows them to channel their efforts without being distracted by handling high-activity job requisitions.

To illustrate this point further, renowned technology companies like *Google* and *Amazon* employ 'sourcers' whose primary responsibility is creatively identifying talent that meets hiring needs. By doing this, recruiters can concentrate on attracting and converting candidates while relying on these experts for candidate identification. Think of them as sports scouts who tirelessly search for promising prospects.

Coaching for Exceptional Interviews

It is essential to provide skills development for hiring managers and interviewers, so they can consistently apply considerations and enhance their abilities in question development, active listening, assessment techniques, and ensuring an exceptional candidate experience during conversations.

Regular group training sessions, self-paced e-learning programs, and knowledge sharing among peers help leaders evolve into evaluators. For instance, *Clorox* has implemented refresher courses where managers exchange creative behavioral questions with one another. This coaching approach prevents skills from deteriorating over time.

Developing Skilled Facilitators
We need to invest in personnel who have the expertise to facilitate assessment centers. These professionals should also be able to lead collaborative debriefing sessions after interviews or assessments. Additionally, they should be skilled in conducting panel interviews, where interviewers assess candidates collectively, and in organizing multi-candidate events (where multiple individuals are evaluated simultaneously).

Incentivize Advocacy
Encourage talent acquisition team members to publish blog posts or speak at local events evangelizing innovative initiatives delivered for business impact. Gaining public recognition for achievements beyond internal metrics fuels further innovation. *Adobe* and *Intuit* incubate recruiter-led special projects converting successes into webinars and conference workshops. Such visibility also aids future talent attraction.

Gain Insights from Related Areas
Explore training programs for recruiters in sales, hospitality, and client services that can be beneficial for talent acquisition teams. For instance, skills in conflict resolution as a mediator can be applied to negotiating job offers. Customer service principles, like providing concierge service can enhance the candidate experience. Embracing forward-thinking allows talent teams to go beyond Human Resources boundaries.

Organizations that aim to change the world understand the importance of investing in recruiting specialists, interviewers, and program leaders who are capable of attracting industry-leading candidates. They recognize that having a sourcing strategy combined with assessment acumen creates an edge. It's crucial to resource talent teams to achieve greatness in recruitment.

The Essence of a Great Recruiter

A great recruiter possesses a unique blend of skills - a deep understanding of the job market, an innate ability to gauge candidate potential, and a talent for fostering meaningful relationships.

Case Study: Alice Thompson, Tech Industry Recruiter

Let's take a look at the story of Alice Thompson, who works as a recruiter in the tech industry. Alice stands out in this field due to her ability to identify talented individuals that others may overlook. She focuses not just on the technical skills but also on a candidate's ability to adapt and grow.

Alice takes an approach by building connections with candidates. She doesn't simply reach out when there's a job opening; she keeps in touch, offering industry insights and career advice. This strategy has helped her establish a network of trust resulting in candidates often approaching her first when they're considering making a change.

The Art of Effective Interviewing

An effective interviewer goes beyond evaluating a candidate's qualifications. They create an environment where candidates can truly showcase their abilities and also assess their fit within the company culture.

Case Study: David Lee, Senior Manager at a Financial Firm
Now let's shift our attention to David Lee, a manager at a firm renowned for his exceptional interview skills. David starts each interview by asking open-ended questions that encourage candidates to share their experiences. This technique allows him to assess not just their competencies but also their problem-solving approach and emotional intelligence.

David pays close attention to how candidates describe past challenges and their role in overcoming them. He looks for indicators of leadership, teamwork, and resilience. His methodical yet empathetic approach to interviewing has helped his firm build a team that is not only skilled but also highly cohesive.

Creating a Culture of Excellent Recruitment
To excel in recruitment, an organization must foster an environment that values and nurtures outstanding recruiting practices. For instance, a cutting-edge technology startup, recognized for its exceptional hiring practices, attributes its success to its recruiter training programs. These programs focus on equipping recruiters to understand the company's technology and culture. Recruiters are also trained in interviewing techniques to effectively evaluate a candidate's skills and cultural alignment.

The startup encourages collaboration between recruiters and hiring managers ensuring a seamless recruitment experience. This partnership guarantees that recruiters have a grasp of the positions they are hiring for and can adeptly convey the company's vision to candidates.

Embracing Diversity, in Recruitment
Exceptional recruiters and interviewers recognize the significance of diversity when building teams. They actively strive to eliminate biases and create an inclusive hiring process.

Case Study: Sara Johnson, Diversity and Inclusion Lead
Sara Johnson, a Diversity and Inclusion Lead at a multinational corporation, has been instrumental in shaping her company's approach to diverse hiring. She implemented training programs on unconscious bias for recruiters and interviewers, helping them understand and mitigate their biases.

In addition, Sara has taken steps to diversify the recruitment pipeline by establishing partnerships with organizations and communities dedicated to fostering diversity in the workforce. These efforts have not only resulted in a diverse pool of hires for the company but have also had a positive impact on its culture, encouraging innovation and facilitating growth.

THE TALENT TECHNOLOGY ECOSYSTEM

Recruiting excellence requires thoughtfully curating and connecting best-of-breed solutions for process-specific impact (CRM, assessments) into a flexible integrated ecosystem tied to core HR platforms (HRIS, Performance management).

Implement CRM and Marketing Automation
Utilize tracking software (ATS) and customer relationship management (CRM) tools designed specifically to manage talent relationships and workflows beyond initial applicant

entries. The CRM system allows for personalized and automated nurturing of candidates, guiding them toward opportunities that align with their backgrounds. Marketing automation functionality enables the execution of campaigns at scale helping to source talent based on emerging priorities.

Administer Assessments Virtually
Procure dedicated skills testing, video interviewing, and assessment platforms tailored to delivering remote evaluations mapped to key competencies. For example, coding challenge platforms like *HackerRank* can be utilized for developer roles while writing tests can be used for communications positions. Ensure that the results from these assessments are seamlessly integrated into hiring manager reviews.

Structure for Point-to-Point Interoperability
As larger HR systems incorporate recruiting tools, there is a growing need for integrated suites. However, it is essential not to prioritize user experience at the expense of the functionality provided by individual solutions that excel in specific use cases. Instead, emphasize data integration, across the ecosystem so that leading platforms can efficiently share insights while preserving the unique benefits offered by specialized tools.

Embrace Specialized Innovation
Stay updated on early-stage startups that are spearheading cutting-edge techniques, which may not easily integrate with existing outdated tools. These startups tackle innovative challenges catering to diverse needs. Examples of niche innovators include *WayUp* (for campus sourcing) *SeekOut* (for diversity pipelines) and *SkillSurvey* (for reference assessments

from ICIMS). It's worth exploring their advancements before they become mainstream.

Analyze and Recommend Holistically

As artificial intelligence becomes more prevalent in talent technology, it is crucial to ensure that recommendation engines applied to areas like job matching or chatbot screening take into consideration candidates holistically. Avoid classifying individuals solely based on attributes without examining their nuanced profiles.

Automate Strategically, Not Excessively

Avoid the notion that automation should replace judgment throughout the recruitment process. Instead, focus on automating rules-driven activities that can benefit from scalability and consistency such as scheduling or screening questionnaires. However, remember to preserve the intelligence required for talent interpretation during interviews and evaluations. Instead of suddenly giving up control, gently steer the direction of a candidate's outcome.

Leverage Predictive Insights

Use data from talent analytics platforms that can predict leadership potential, retention risk, and performance. Consider these insights along with past achievements when evaluating candidates for a role. Recommendation algorithms can then guide the next steps without completely replacing the recruiter's judgment.

Ensuring Adequate Security Measures

While the convenience and collaborative benefits of adopting cloud hosting services are significant, it is crucial to acknowledge that talent records contain applicant information. Therefore it is necessary to implement controls such as data encryption, IAM role-based policies, permissions, MFA-protected access, and event auditing to ensure compliance and protect against exposure.

Promoting Interoperability
Considering the history of recruiting solutions catering to specific needs, it is vital to actively pursue the modernization of integration capabilities and data portability. This will enable connectivity across systems and ecosystems inherited from previous implementations. Expanding API functionality, utilizing metadata templates, and synchronizing profiles can contribute to achieving composite environment harmony.

Balancing Technological Proficiency in Recruitment
Proficiency in technology plays a role in recruitment processes. However striking a balance between innovation, specialization, human judgment, and automation is equally important, for elevating the ecosystem. By combining these elements, recruiters can achieve an approach that maximizes efficiency and effectiveness.

In concluding this exploration of building a recruitment program, let's revisit the story of Emily Johnson at Orion Tech in San Francisco. Her journey which encompassed the three aspects discussed earlier, provides an understanding of what it takes to transform a company's talent acquisition process.

One key factor in Emily's success was her dedication to revitalizing Orion Tech's recruitment strategy. She invested time analyzing market trends, evaluating the company's hiring needs, and aligning the recruitment approach with long-term business objectives. Her method combined data-driven insights with a focus on candidate experience.

Emily took an approach by building relationships with candidates well in advance. This not only established a talent pipeline but also positioned Orion Tech as an appealing employer within the tech industry. Emily's efforts in diversifying recruitment channels yielded results attracting individuals from diverse backgrounds and areas of expertise.

Additionally, part of Emily's strategy involved prioritizing a candidate's experience. She implemented streamlined application processes, transparent communication practices, and engaging interactions. These changes led to an uptick in positive feedback from candidates, even those who weren't ultimately hired, bolstering Orion Tech's reputation in the job market.

Emily's second phase of the strategy focused on her team. The recruiters and interviewers represented the side of Orion Tech's hiring process. She carefully selected recruiters who not only possessed talent-sourcing skills but also embraced Orion Tech culture wholeheartedly. She invested in their growth ensuring they stayed up to date with the tools and techniques in talent acquisition.

Emily also revamped the interview process. She trained her interviewers to conduct empathetic interviews by paying attention to both the technical expertise and cultural compatibility of candidates. Her team became adept at asking questions by actively listening and evaluating candidates based on standardized criteria.

These efforts revolutionized recruitment at Orion Tech. The interviewers proficient in assessing candidates beyond their resumes, could identify individuals who not only met the requirements of the current position but also showed potential for future growth within the company.

The final aspect of Emily's strategy involved integrating technology into the recruitment process. She had successfully developed a technology ecosystem that streamlined the recruitment process from sourcing to onboarding. To enhance efficiency, Emily introduced an Applicant Tracking System (ATS) that automated tasks allowing her team to focus more on strategic aspects of recruitment. In addition, she employed AI-powered sourcing tools that helped identify candidates expanding their talent search, beyond job seekers.

For interviews, Emily invested in top-notch video conferencing tools and virtual reality setups for immersive job previews. These tools not only made the interview process more efficient but also made it accessible to candidates worldwide.

One of Emily's decisions was incorporating data analytics into their recruitment practices. By analyzing recruitment data, she gained insights into the effectiveness of sourcing channels, candidate behaviors, and overall hiring process efficiency. This data-driven approach enabled the refinement and improvement of their recruitment strategies.

As Emily looked back on her journey, she felt a sense of pride and accomplishment. Under her guidance, Orion Tech's recruitment process became a benchmark in the tech industry. Her strategy went beyond simply filling positions, it was focused on building a team that drove innovation and fostered growth at Orion Tech.

The recruitment program she created demonstrated her belief that a combination of strategy, skilled team members, and technology could revolutionize talent acquisition.

Emily's story is an example of organizations seeking to enhance their recruitment process, blending vision, personal connections, and technological innovation. Her experience at Orion Tech highlights the importance of taking an approach to building a top-notch recruiting program that balances both the art and science of talent acquisition.

As we conclude this chapter, it becomes evident that the journey toward creating a recruiting program is ongoing and ever-evolving. The landscape of talent acquisition constantly changes, presenting challenges and opportunities. However, with a foundation in planning, a team consisting of exceptional recruiters and interviewers, and the integration of technology, any organization can attract, hire, and retain the necessary talent to thrive in today's competitive market. Emily Johnson's story exemplifies the effectiveness of this approach while serving as a guiding beacon for recruitment endeavors.

CONCLUSION

Our recruiting excellence journey spanned numerous disciplines - from strategic sourcing to candidate assessment to process improvement. I appreciate you joining me to impart hard-won lessons from the front lines of talent acquisition leadership. Now, let's recap key milestones explored to cement comprehensive capabilities elevating your organization's talent attraction maturity.

We started by focusing on the basics of achieving greatness in recruitment – understanding your talent requirements thoroughly before launching recruitment campaigns. Considerate analysis of needs and profiling of target candidates help coordinate efforts, for suitability and motivation. Adopting an approach enabled us to fill our buckets through ingenuity and determination.

Next, we delved into evaluation techniques that go beyond interviews and resumes to gather insights into candidates' competencies in action. Customized assessments provide data that supports decision-making. Implementing feedback loops helps bridge any perception gaps. Ultimately, aligning evaluations tightly to success predictors, mitigating bias risks, delivers informed candidate conclusions.

After attracting and assessing talent, our focus shifted towards optimizing the recruitment experience from start to finish. By putting ourselves in the shoes of the candidates, and understanding their journey, we were able to identify areas where friction could arise. Refining touchpoints with care and clarity strengthens the impression of our employer brand. Additionally, engaging candidates with content that aligns with our values further enhances their connection with us.

To strengthen our recruiting strategy we also addressed the intricacies of sourcing for niches. Thoroughly mapping out capabilities proved crucial before implementing outreach approaches. Captivating messages have the power to captivate niche audiences by being relevant. Establishing connections with communities helps discover opportunities for growth that competitors may not explore.

Switching gears, we then delved into the importance of analyzing data. Consistently tracking metrics allows us to establish benchmarks for analysis uncovering performance gaps that might otherwise go unnoticed. Advanced techniques such as predictive hiring demand modeling and text mining can provide insights that inform data-driven decision-making effectively. However, it's crucial to act on these insights for them to have an impact.

Next, we discussed strategies for promoting openings. By orchestrating channels, nurturing campaigns, leveraging peer referrals, and modern community building, convey passion for possibilities attracting aspirational candidates, beyond passive job description. Compelling and innovative content highlights our authentic company culture in a way that resonates with candidates. Monitoring analytics ensures that our efforts are tied to results.

Lastly, we explored elevating complete talent programs comprehensively addressing strategy developments, interview training, and technology ecosystems holistically. Each aspect of recruitment demands its own set of skills. When we align these skills consistently, our organization's capabilities increase significantly. Success is achieved through orchestration across all segments; no individual effort can stand alone.

Of course, we only scratched the surface on topics that deserve deeper examination individually on their own merits. However, this interactive journey has equipped you with talent insights that you can immediately put into action while also inspiring further mastery.

I hope that the enthusiasm we have sparked together will inspire your teams to recruit and drive business performance through valuable partnerships with people.

Finally, let us not forget that our primary goal is to connect professionals with fulfilling opportunities that benefit both their careers and the companies they join. That is why we are dedicated to this craft. It is our responsibility to continuously refine our approaches and elevate recruitment from being a cost-center necessity to being a driving force for organizations where purpose and profits converge.

Now go forth. Unleash the catalyst within you! Our world needs recruiters who are committed to nurturing talent and exploring possibilities. I am excited to hear about your successes in the coming days. Stay courageous my friends.

THANK YOU

As I come to the end of this journey, I just wanted to say a thank you to all you readers for coming along with me on this exploration of finding top-notch talent. Your curiosity and involvement are what give purpose to this book.

I am truly grateful for all the encouragement, input, and wisdom that has been exchanged throughout this process of writing this book. My wish is that this book has given you some insights and tactics to step up your recruitment game.

I'd be thrilled to keep chatting and getting to know you. Don't hesitate to connect with me on LinkedIn at https://www.linkedin.com/in/anirbanbiswas/ - Share your reflections, stories, and any meaningful conversation this book may have inspired.

Let's keep the dialogue going and continue to grow and learn from each other in the dynamic world of recruitment.

www.ingramcontent.com/pod-product-compliance
Lightning Source LLC
Chambersburg PA
CBHW031630210526
45464CB00004B/1832